7 Things You Better Have Nailed Down

Before All Hell Breaks Loose

Other Books by Robert Wolgemuth

Dad's Bible

The Most Important Place on Earth

She Calls Me Daddy

The Most Important Year in a Man's Life with Mark DeVries

Daddy@Work

From Daddy with Love

Just Daddy and Me

Notes in *The Devotional Bible for Dads*

Men of the Bible with Ann Spangler

Prayers from a Dad's Heart

What's in the Bible with R. C. Sproul

The Great Hymns of Our Faith Series

7

THINGS YOU BETTER
HAVE NAILED DOWN

BEFORE ALL HELL BREAKS LOOSE

Robert Wolgemuth

THOMAS NELSON
Since 1798

NASHVILLE   DALLAS   MEXICO CITY   RIO DE JANEIRO   BEIJING

Published in Nashville, Tennessee, by Thomas Nelson. Thomas Nelson is a registered trademark of Thomas Nelson, Inc.

Thomas Nelson, Inc. titles may be purchased in bulk for educational, business, fund-raising, or sales promotional use. For information, please e-mail SpecialMarkets@ThomasNelson.com.

Library of Congress Cataloging-in-Publication Data

Wolgemuth, Robert D.
  7 things you better have nailed down before all hell breaks loose / Robert Wolgemuth.
    p. cm.
  Includes bibliographical references.
  ISBN 978-0-7852-2169-2 (hardcover)
  ISBN 978-0-7852-8956-2 (trade paper)
    1. Theology, Doctrinal. I. Title. II. Title: Seven things you better have nailed down before all Hell breaks loose.
  BT75.3.W65 2007
  230—dc22   2006032848

Printed in the United States of America

08 09 10 11 12 RRD 5 4 3 2 1

DEDICATION

Andrew Donald Wolgemuth

Erik Samuel Wolgemuth

Nephews, colleagues, friends

"Blessed is the man,
Who walks not in the counsel of the ungodly,
Nor stands in the path of sinners,
Nor sits in the seat of the scornful;
But his delight is in the law of the LORD,
And in His law he meditates day and night.
He shall be like a tree
Planted by the rivers of water,
That brings forth its fruit in its season,
Whose leaf also shall not wither;
And whatsoever he does shall prosper."

—Psalm 1:1–3

Contents

Preface

The first time my husband Mark and I were introduced to the material in this book it was being taught by our Sunday school teacher, Robert Wolgemuth.

We were happily married with two young children, living the American dream. We listened carefully to each of the seven things Robert was talking about, and I took notes. Mark and I agreed that these were good things for people like us to know—young and healthy, with our futures ahead of us. Life was good.

But in the fall of 2004, I went to the doctor concerned about the lump I had found in my breast. We hoped it would turn out to be nothing. It *wasn't* nothing. On November 5, I received the diagnosis: stage IV metastatic breast cancer with three cancerous spots on my liver. From the deepest crevices of my soul, all hell had broken loose.

With the news, Mark and I experienced an emotional freefall—a tailspin—beyond telling. It was official and there would be no turning back. We had many decisions to make. The first and most important concerned our faith, that it would be strong enough to help us *really* walk the path we had professed and helped others to know.

Our parents had given us the gift beyond all gifts as children, a sound understanding of and love for God. With the essentials that Robert's teaching had *nailed down* for us, we had a place to land. A solid place that did not move. This foundation and the hope that it brought literally came from the words you're about to read in this book.

The God of creation, our merciful Father, sustained our frightened hearts. Words we had read from the Bible came into sharp focus. New readings from the Scriptures jumped off the pages and embraced us. In a way that I cannot fully describe, Jesus held us with arms of comfort and assurance. And God's people rallied with the kind of encouragement and help that we could never have imagined.

Here I was—thirty-seven years old, a mother of two very young children and a wife to a wonderful husband who loved me—facing the horrors of cancer and the ravages of intense treatment. Amazingly, though, because of the faith that sustained me, the things that had been nailed down in my heart, I was even able to encourage others who had come to encourage me.

I could go on and on about how important I believe this material is, but I'll let you read the following pages and see that for yourself.

For Mark and me, this may or may not have been the greatest crisis in our lives—only God knows that. But I'm thankful for all the times that came before and will certainly come after because I know that God is my rock and my salvation. That will never change. His grace and mercies are new each day.

— Mrs. Pam Oldham
Orlando, FL

Introduction

It was fall 1974. My wife, Bobbie, and I had been married for four and a half years. Our first child, Missy, had just celebrated her third birthday, and Bobbie was expecting our second baby.

Over three weeks past the due date, Bobbie finally went into labor on October 24. Folks had told us that the second child's birth was always easier. Good news for Bobbie, who had spent fourteen hours in labor with Missy. But there were complications. This baby was in breech position, sitting upright in the womb rather than in the normal head-down position.

After almost eighteen hours of intense labor, Julie was born. Because it was necessary for the doctor to give Bobbie general anesthetic, I could not be present for the delivery and was forced to stand in a small alcove just outside the operating room.

Not a moment too soon, Dr. James Eggers walked through the door. "You have a little girl," he said, then added with a sigh, "but there's a problem."

With no other explanation, he turned and walked quickly back into the OR.

Time stood still. What did I believe? What could I hold on to? What would sustain me? Where could I safely stand?

What happened is difficult to fully describe, but I had an overwhelming sense that I was, in the words of the hymn, "standing in [God's] presence, on holy ground." As I stood alone, outside the operating room, that reassuring presence was very, very real.

Scriptures came to mind: "He who dwells in the secret place of the Most High shall abide under the shadow of the Almighty. I will say of the LORD, 'He is my refuge and my fortress; my God, in Him I will trust'" (Ps. 91:1–2).

Lyrics from a hymn long ago tucked into my memory rhythmically paced through my head.

> When through the deep waters I call you to go,
> The rivers of sorrow shall not overflow;
> For I will be with you, your troubles to bless,
> And sanctify to you your deepest distress.[1]

Sitting on a cold, vinyl waiting-room chair at Holy Family Hospital in Des Plaines, Illinois, these words visited me like old friends.

Ironically, I didn't memorize these verses to have something to turn to when the doctor gave me the news no father wanted to hear. How could I have known? But they immediately reminded me of a safe place—the only place—on which I could stand when there was nothing else. A strong place, when it seemed as though all hell had broken loose.

Within an hour the operating-room door opened again, and Dr. Eggers walked toward me. "Your little girl's right leg is limp and is not responding to stimulation. We don't know if the problem is isolated with her leg or if it's central . . . neurological."

For the next two years, our lives were filled with multiple visits to pediatric specialists whose diagnoses ranged from intrauterine polio to congenital nerve damage. No certain diagnosis was ever established.[2]

Time for the Basics

It's been over thirty years since Dr. Eggers gave me the news—thirty years of my own struggle to nail down those things that do not change. I'm talking about things that, in a pluralistic culture, continue to fall into the growing and unpopular and vigorously contested category of absolute and inarguable truth—truth, however, that literally explodes to the surface when all hell breaks loose. Truth that may have been the subject of ridicule the day before suddenly becomes the truth that sustains and gives hope.

A Sunday School Series with the Word *Hell* in It

In the late '80s, a friend encouraged me to teach a Sunday school series about the unchangeable basics of our Christian faith. I remember thinking that selecting a handful of nonnegotiables to present to our class sounded like a good idea. *Why not equip ourselves for the flames of persecution or the trauma of heartbreak?* I thought to myself.

As a hopeless "title-maker," I began looking around for an appropriate name for the series. Bobbie and I discussed several ideas. Then I remembered a phrase I had heard many years before . . . something about "truth getting nailed down before all hell broke loose."

"Let's call the series, 'Seven Things You Better Have Nailed Down Before All Hell Breaks Loose,'" I said. Bobbie liked the idea.

Over the years, I have taught this material many times. But what started as a somewhat playful title has become desperately serious. All hell breaking loose is as predictable as the sun setting tonight and rising tomorrow morning. Since ancient times, philosophers, ministers, scholars, and world leaders have thought their generation was careening into chaos.

And the proliferation of new technologies guarantees instantaneous, worldwide communication. No tragedy goes unreported. You and I need to be ready . . . for anything.

Regardless of how many years pass between the time I'm writing these words and the time you read them, the headlines from this morning's newspaper probably renewed that sinking feeling in your soul. That sensation that you know trouble is brewing everywhere . . . politically, socially, economically, militarily. Beyond the situation in the world, maybe you're experiencing serious trouble yourself or you sense that it could be just around the corner.

The best thing that you and I can do is to visit—or revisit—the basics. We need to prepare for all hell breaking loose by building a foundation on which we can safely stand.

The Following Pages Are for You

I don't know if you've just emerged from a crisis, are currently dealing with a crisis, or are preparing for something unknown just around the corner, but the pages that follow will give you perspective, comfort you, and prepare you for whatever difficulty or tragedy coming your way.

This book is not intended to frighten you with the specter of awful things to come, but to remind you as you get ready for your clutch turn at bat . . . to keep you steady on the thinnest of strings.

You may be a devout Christian or a relative newcomer to religious things . . . someone who is genuinely curious about issues of faith. You may live in North America where 90 percent of people claim they believe in God or you may be somewhere else in the world. Whoever and wherever you are, these pages make the assumption that you want more—more information about what it is that you believe and a greater level of intentionality about what you want to do with that information.

My hope is that the following chapters will be understandable, instructive, and helpful.

God bless you.
Dr. Robert Wolgemuth
Orlando, Florida

BEFORE ALL HELL
BREAKS LOOSE . . .

One of my closest friends can't stand Major League Baseball. I have tried to talk to him about the physical challenges and intricacies of the game, but his response is always the same.

"Borrrrrring," he says smiling.

My friend's disdain for the game has had no affect on me. Whether in person at a game or watching on TV, I have always been captured by the sport. The remarkable skill of a pitcher as he throws a baseball ninety miles an hour, sixty feet, six inches away from home plate with the precision of a surgeon, or the catlike silkiness of an infielder scooping up a ground ball and rocketing it to first base.

I'm also taken with the skill of a batter, actually catching up with the speeding baseball and hitting it 450 feet into the stands. Success is so elusive that even the best of hitters fail more often than they succeed.

If you're like my friend and are eager for me to move along to something you care about, please hang on for a couple more minutes. There's a point to my talking about baseball.

Clutch Hitting

One of the baseball issues that has been discussed and researched over the past few years has to do with how certain batters do when the outcome of the game is on the line and the batter's success could mean the difference between his team winning or losing . . . *clutch hitting.*

It seems that some hitters are considered to be more proficient when the game depends on it than when they step into the batter's box under more ordinary circumstances.

Because baseball has, since its inception, been populated by geeky statisticians, a serious controversy has arisen over whether or not any batter—today or throughout the history of the game—has actually done better in the clutch. Intense scrutiny has been given to the minutia of statistics about players who have been known to be great at clutch hitting.[1]

The results may surprise you.

The evidence is conclusive: what a player does under specific game-dependent pressure is exactly what he does at other times. There may be a season or two when a hitter is more productive in the clutch, but the statistics over his lifetime always average out.

A batter is a batter is a batter. What he does under stress is what he does every other day. If he's terrific on those ordinary days, he'll be terrific under pressure. If he's not very good day to day, he won't be any good when the game is on the line.

Given this information, how would you coach a hitter who wants to be better in the clutch? How would you help him be dependable and confident when the game is on the line?

That's right. You'd teach him to improve under normal circumstances . . . before he's in win-or-lose situations. The better his skill has been honed for the ordinary, the more ready he'll be when it really counts.

Baseball and Hell Breaking Loose?

Although the title of this book sounds a bit like a wailing siren, it's really as simple as the principle behind clutch hitting.

If you and I want to be prepared for the inevitable difficulties, challenges, and even tragedies that life will throw at us, we need to learn how to "survive" the normal. We need to nail down essential truth *before* all hell breaks loose.

Final Instructions from The King

Nothing pulls back the curtain on what you and I have nailed down like death, especially the specter of our own demise.

When King David was about to die, he laid down his own list of things he wanted his son Solomon to have nailed down.

> Now the days of David drew near that he should die, and he charged Solomon his son, saying: "I go the way of all the earth; be strong, therefore, and prove yourself a man. And keep the charge of the LORD your God: to walk in His ways, to keep His statutes, His commandments, His judgments, and His testimonies, as it is written in the Law of Moses, that you may prosper in all that you do and wherever you turn."[2]

Can you imagine Solomon looking around for a piece of paper and a pencil? "Let's see," he must have whispered to himself as he wrote. "Walk in God's ways, keep His statutes, His commandments, His judgments, and His testimonies."

The instructions from David to his son were thorough and specific. A veritable cornucopia of things he wanted Solomon to nail down. The promise

David gave to Solomon if he did these things made the rigors of following them well worth it. "You [will have] prosperity in all that you do and wherever you turn."

A New Way of Turning

You and I understand the meaning of the word *prosperity*. But what about the expression "wherever you turn"?

Here's a new way of looking at this old promise.

Spinning things—turning things—have always been a fascination to me. As a young boy, yo-yos and spinning tops were among my favorite toys. As a teenager I was introduced to the magic of the gyroscope . . . where spinning things and physics joined hands. I don't remember if I saved my own money for my first gyroscope or if someone gave it to me, but the toy captured my imagination.

About the size of a small apple, my gyroscope was a spinning top resting inside a simple wire frame. With a piece of string wound around the spine of the top, I pulled with all my might, making the top come to life in a whir. Then I'd take the string and hold it in between my outstretched hands. One of my brothers would set the spinning gyroscope on the string and, like a skilled tightrope walker in the circus, the gyroscope would balance perfectly on the string. Balance was achieved because of something going on inside.

Solomon's obedience to his father's specific instructions were going to prosper him wherever he turned. "Remember to do *all* of these things," David said, "and you will be prosperous wherever you turn." Although drawing a comparison with a gyroscope may seem strange to you, it's an incredibly important principle to learn.

Let me show you how a gyroscope works.[3]

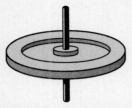

A gyroscope is at rest in a zero-gravity environment. It consists of a simple smooth (frictionless) disc, and a metal pin running through the center.

The disc is not spinning. Using your finger, you push down on a spot near the edge of the disc.

As expected, the disc tilts around its center.

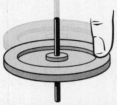

Get the disc spinning at a high rate, and do the same experiment again. This time the whole disc moves down without changing orientation, even though we pushed it near the edge. How did it do that?

Let's do the experiment again, this time using a red marker.

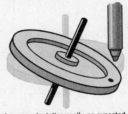

The disc changes orientation easily, as expected, and the red spot on the disc shows where it was pushed.

Do it with the disc rapidly spinning. As soon as the marker touches the disc, a red circle appears all the way around the disc. This red circle shows all the points where the disc is being pushed down. The whole disc will move down, just as you should expect it to move when you push it down on all points of the red circle!

Regardless of the pressure it faces, a spinning gyroscope cannot be thrown off balance. Now you know why this is true.

At this moment, our life situations fall into one of three categories. We're either just coming out of a crisis, in the middle of a crisis, or about to have a crisis head our way.

Like the illustration of the finger pressing on the edge of the gyroscope, something or someone has just tried to tilt our lives. It's pressing down on us, or is about to come crashing in.

Although he probably didn't understand much about physics, King David was admonishing his son to hold steady, regardless of what was happening to him. "Walk in God's ways, keep His statutes, His commandments, His judgments, and His testimonies."

The result of obeying his dad's admonition would provide Solomon with prosperity "wherever he turned."

Batter Up ... When It's Your Turn

You hear the ambulance siren, as you have many times before. Only this time, instead of the sound waning, its reverberation gets louder and LOUDER. It's headed for *your* house. The moment seems surreal, as though you're in a time warp, disjointed from reality. Things that just seconds before were so important now disappear into irrelevance.

The telephone rings, and you answer, with no idea what is about to happen to your life. As soon as you say hello, the caller delivers the news—the last thing you expected—or wanted—to hear. You stand there in body-numbing disbelief. One of the most cherished people in the world to you is gone. There wasn't even time for a final good-bye.

There's a knock on your front door. You weren't expecting anyone, at least not that you could remember. The man seems overdressed. Perhaps he's a salesman. You're a little surprised when he speaks your name, lifting his tone at the end as if it's a question. You nod, and the man hands you a legal document, then a clipboard with a paper for you to sign, acknowledging receipt of the document. You knew your marriage was in trouble—your spouse *has* seemed more distant than ever—but you hadn't predicted anything this final. You scribble your name, step back into your home, and close the door, staggering in disbelief. You can hardly breathe.

You're at thirty-seven thousand feet, clipping along at five hundred miles an hour. Your laptop is open, and you're catching up on some correspondence, when you feel the plane tremble slightly. *Just a little rough air*, you say to yourself. But when it happens again, the trembling is a little more violent. You look around at the other passengers. Most of them haven't looked up. Then there's a loud crack, and the plane drops suddenly, pitching first to the left, then sharply to the right. As the flight attendants rush to their seats, the captain announces, "There's been an equipment failure on our aircraft, and we're looking for the nearest airfield for an emergency landing. Remove everything from your lap and prepare yourself." Some passengers cry out, but most, like you, lean forward quietly and wrap their arms around their legs. You're not sure what's happening, but you know it is serious. Maybe perilous.

You've heard the expression. Now it's real: *All hell has broken loose*. For you. What are you going to do?

There's a good chance that one of these things—or something similar—has already happened to you. You know the sense of desperation. There's nothing you can do about what's happening. But it is. You feel naked and vulnerable—and very afraid.

What did you do? Where did your mind take you? Was it a freefall, or was there something to hang on to?

Even if you're not experiencing one of these panic-producing events right now, go ahead and think back to one you've had before. What did it feel like? What was racing through your consciousness? Can you remember what you did in the face of this unexpected crisis?

History is peppered with accounts of ordinary people, like you and me, who have faced indescribable crisis. As a boy, I was enthralled by their stories. Here were people who stood strong in the face of their own personal "hell breaking loose" moments. What they did was unbelievable.

A Young Boy and a Book

In one corner of my childhood living room sat a large upholstered chair, nestled beside a brown stone fireplace. Behind the chair was a small bookcase, built smartly into a short corner wall—a knee wall.

The triangular space on the backside of the chair made an ideal place—a fort—for a small boy to lie on his stomach and read a book. The youngster was me, and the book was *Foxe's Book of Martyrs*.

My minister dad had purchased this book with specific intentions. His children would need to get ready. All hell was going to break loose for America.

The Cold War was at full volume. The Soviet Union was brandishing its weaponry, its rhetoric strident and brash. "We will bury you," Nikita Khrushchev had said to a group of Western ambassadors. And Lt. Gen. William K. Harrison, an army commander during the Korean War and a friend of my dad's, had told him, in no uncertain terms, that our generation would face persecution.

It was in the late 1950s—I was ten years old—when I first met Thomas Bilney in the pages of *Foxe's Book of Martyrs*. Thomas was a student at the University of Cambridge in the sixteenth century. He had shown a remarkable love of learning. And he was the kind of man I wanted to grow up to be.

I remember being drawn by his grit and determination. A gentle and humble lad, Thomas studied law and religion. He was particularly fascinated with the Bible and the claims of Christianity. His interest turned to passion as he became a devoted follower of Jesus Christ.

After graduation, many of his friends pursued "respectable" professions. But Thomas and his friend Thomas Arthur devoted their lives to telling others about their love for God. Their mission took them to prison cells and to the poorest areas of London. At first, Thomas Bilney preached at small gatherings in private homes, but as the quality and power of his preaching and teaching grew, so did the size of his congregation. He filled churches with compelling messages of God's judgment and grace. "Salvation is through Christ alone," he preached. "Rites, rituals, and work are mere emptiness unless they are done in Christ."[4]

One day, while traveling through Norwich, a city fifty miles northeast of London, Thomas stopped to visit a woman in her home. He gave her a copy of a Tyndale Bible, translated in English. He knew this was against the law.

For unlawful distribution of the sacred Scripture, Thomas Bilney was captured and thrown in prison. After examination and condemnation by the church, and thoroughly unwilling to alter his actions or recant his beliefs, Thomas was sentenced to die at the stake.

August 19, 1531, was a windy day, and as the first large flame flared in his face, singeing his beard and burning off his eyebrows and lashes, Thomas did not flinch. As people gathered to watch the spectacle, the gentle Thomas Bilney shouted, "Jesus!" and "I believe!" Soon the flames had taken his life, his clothing burned from his body, his naked head charred. One of the executioners removed the staple from the chain fastened to the back of the stake, and Thomas's body fell into the fire and was soon completely consumed.

The heart in my small body pounded with such fury as I read this story that I could feel my temples throb. I was overwhelmed by Thomas's courage—his fearlessness at the specter of his imminent execution, simply because he loved and believed in Christ. And I remembered his dying words as the flames burned him. His shout of "Jesus!" identified his Savior. "I believe!" let all those present know that no external forces would be able to extinguish what he knew to be true. No one—no terror—would have the power to change his mind. For Thomas, all hell had broken loose. And he had faced it with confidence.

Where did this stalwart confidence come from? How did he die with such certainty and poise?

Besides Thomas Bilney, *Foxe's Book of Martyrs* introduced me to others. People with funny names, like Polycarp, Chrysostom, Denisa, Wycliffe, and other men . . . and women and even children who died unspeakable deaths for their belief in Christ.

The irony for me was that these people died because they *chose* to—the hell they faced could have been avoided. Unwilling to secure their own release by renouncing their love for Jesus Christ or condemning their passion to preach, some of these martyrs sang hymns as their bodies burned at the stake. Some prayed aloud for their executioners as swords impaled their bodies. Others quoted Scripture as wild dogs tore at them. Like obedient apprentices, some held sharp chisels against their own arms, while their torturers hammered the chisels that severed their limbs . . . all the while telling these monsters that God loved them. And forgave them.

> *The hell they endured stripped away their doubt, sealing their determination.*

What fascinated me back then—and still does today—is that the very torture that these saints faced, galvanized their beliefs. The hell they endured stripped away their doubt, sealing their determination. Their faith was enough.

A Few Years Later

When I was in college, almost ten years after my childhood encounters with the martyrs, there were other brave men to meet. Men my age. An understanding of why the martyrs' stories had stirred me so powerfully showed up in the lives of people I actually knew. Like Scott.

It was a warm, lazy Sunday afternoon in the spring of 1968. I was a junior at Taylor University. As I walked down the hall toward my dormitory room, I saw an uncommon thing, even for our notorious wing. An Indiana state trooper was standing in front of someone's door, knocking. As I approached, he turned and asked, "Do you know where Scott Hawkins is?"

I had seen Scott and his girlfriend, Jenny, leave campus in his car several hours before. The officer asked if I would be willing to look for Scott and deliver an important message to him.

"Mr. Hawkins's mother and sister and brother have been in a serious automobile accident," he began, speaking formally, precisely, and without emotion. "They're in the Wabash Community Hospital, and Mr. Hawkins needs to get there as quickly as possible."

Promising to find Scott, I agreed to give him the news. The officer thanked me, turned, and walked away, disappearing behind the door at the end of the hall.

The frantic search for Scott and Jenny ended about thirty minutes later when I drove past them as they were pulling onto campus. Waving them down, I dashed from my car to tell them the trooper's news and directive. At first Scott thought I was joking. But the look on my face told him this was real. He said good-bye to Jenny, jumped into my car, and we sped off.

Almost two hours after the officer had delivered the news, Scott and I approached an unpretentious, vine-covered building. The lighted sign in the yard read Wabash Community Hospital. The front door was locked, but a small sign pasted to the door led us to the Please Ring after Hours button on the brick wall, just a few feet away.

The night nurse cracked the door slightly and asked our names. "This is Scott Hawkins," I said, nodding toward my friend. She quickly opened the door, and we walked into the small lobby. "You need to report to the nurses' station on the second floor," she said, pointing us in the direction of a single elevator.

Scott and I rode to the second floor in silence, exactly as we had during the two-hour drive from Taylor. Outside the elevator, the floor in the dark hallway glistened like a polished mirror, reflecting the fluorescent lights above the nurses' station. Approaching the counter, we passed a gurney pushed against the wall. A young boy lay there, a sheet pulled up to his bandaged chin. From the bridge of his nose to the top of his head he was wrapped in white gauze. The boy was sleeping. I recognized him as Scott's little brother, Tim. Focused on speaking to the attending nurse, Scott had not noticed him.

The nurse directed Scott to a room a few doors away. I followed a few steps behind. When his mother saw him from her bed, she burst into tears and reached for him. Scott leaned across the bed and held her.

Suddenly uncomfortable, I stepped back into the hall and returned to the nurses' station.

"How's Scott's sister?" I asked. "Where is she?" The nurse looked up from her work but did not speak. She knew that I wasn't Scott and felt no obligation to give me any information. I remember feeling embarrassed that I had asked.

I spotted a chair in the dark hallway a few feet away and sat down. This was the first time I had been alone since finding Scott on the other side of campus.

Scott Hawkins was the most committed Christian young man I knew. His father had died of colon cancer less than six months before. Now his mother and little brother lay in hospital beds, broken and bruised. His sister, Shelley, lying in intensive care, would never regain consciousness.

Leaning forward, my hands cupped under my chin, I remember being filled with a haunting unrest mixed with awe . . . not unlike the emotions I felt as a youngster reading the book about the martyrs.

Questions came flooding in: *Is there something deep inside me that would enable me to survive if this were happening to me? Would my faith—my beliefs—hold up under this kind of crushing blow?* Like Thomas Bilney, Scott seemed ready to face it. The horror, the pain, the loss. He was certainly broken by what was happening, but his gentle calm—the serenity I saw in him—was visible.

In the silence, I concluded that I *wasn't* ready if this were to happen to me. But in that moment, I resolved that I would do whatever it took to *get* ready. Nothing else in my world mattered.

Having grown up in a solid Christian home, I had deftly sidestepped the need to become spiritually independent, simply making my parents' beliefs my own. But no more. I was finished living the faith of a fair-weather, spiritually childish adolescent. I knew that it was time to grow up . . . time to become a man.

Time to read another Book about great people.

A Handful of Bible Heroes

The Bible is filled with stories of men and women who are much like my boyhood heroes from *Foxe's Book of Martyrs*, people who faced unthinkable odds—some unexpected and some of their own choosing. Many are listed in the book of Hebrews, chapter 11, the New Testament's "Hall of Faith." If you look at this list of saints through the prism of "all hell breaking loose," you'll see what I mean:

Abraham is told to leave everything—and everyone—familiar and move. And he has no idea where he's going. But he goes.[5]

After a lifetime of barrenness, a postmenopausal Sarah is told she is going to have a baby boy . . . and that a nation will be established through him.[6] She almost crumbles under the pressure. Almost.

Later, Abraham is told to lift the knife and sacrifice Isaac, the son of promise.[7] He obeys.

The writer to the Hebrews lists others, like Abel, Enoch, Isaac, Jacob,

Joseph, Moses, Rahab, Gideon, Barak, Samson, Jephthah, David, and Samuel. Read their accounts and you will see shades of *Foxe's*: torture, mocking, scourges, destitution, affliction, and torment.

Noah, one of my three favorite Bible heroes, is named. Another favorite, Daniel, "stopped the mouth of lions."[8] But a third Bible hero, Stephen, isn't mentioned at all. Perhaps the author had him in mind when he penned the words describing those "of whom the world was not worthy."[9]

Before we meet Stephen, Jesus has ascended to heaven following His resurrection. He had challenged His followers to "be witnesses [about Him] in Jerusalem, and in all Judea and Samaria, and to the end of the earth."[10] Taking their charge seriously, the disciples were traveling and preaching all across the known world. But there was a snag.

As churches were being established, there was a growing awareness that some in the communities were suffering. Though God's Word was being preached and people were being spiritually fed, the disciples had a problem. There were converts who had physical needs that were being overlooked.

Someone needed to be appointed to serve the temporal needs of the people. We aren't told exactly how they made their selections, but the first person they chose was Stephen, "a man full of faith and the Holy Spirit."[11]

As sometimes happens when a remarkable person steps forward and finds success—even in serving—some pious, easily threatened religious leaders were swept away by waves of jealousy. One day, a handful of temple thugs attacked Stephen and dragged him before the Sanhedrin, seventy-one of the most powerful Jews in the region. Like Jesus, Stephen was accused of blasphemy by a band of liars who stepped forward to tell stories about what Stephen was preaching. "We heard him say that this Jesus of Nazareth will destroy this temple and change our customs," they reported.[12]

Here was Stephen, selflessly tending to the needs of widows and orphans, yet falsely charged with speaking *against* the God he loved—the very One he was serving. The accusations were outrageous.

No doubt Stephen knew these men were gunning for him. And they would not be satisfied until he was silenced, one way or another. He *had* to know the fate that awaited him if he spoke up for Jesus in their presence.

Then the high priest made the biggest mistake of his storied career. He opened his mouth. "Are these things so?" he asked. And how many times during the minutes that followed do you suspect the high priest wished he could have withdrawn that question?

For Stephen, all hell was about to break loose. What would he do? He could have escaped. An admission of bad judgment and a promised adjustment in his behavior is what his enemies wanted. If Stephen had acquiesced, he would have been released.

Instead, he looked into the faces of abject hypocrisy—seventy-one men with the power to execute him—and spoke. With tedious precision and skill, Stephen disrobed their false piety.

Over the next several minutes, beginning with the account of Abraham, their spiritual father, Stephen summarized God's dealings with His people throughout Jewish history. "Time and time again, patriarchs and prophets were rejected and persecuted," he railed.

The gathered council was well versed in the familiar stories of many of their heroes. In spite of themselves, they were enraptured with Stephen's grasp of their beloved heritage. But the whole presentation, a brilliantly conceived treatise on the authenticity of Jesus the Messiah, was a dazzling setup.

"You're just like them," Stephen boomed. "You bullheaded bigots, deliberately rejecting the Holy Spirit. You're just like your forefathers who killed every man who prophesied the coming of the very one you've been waiting for. You've done it again with Jesus of Nazareth . . . and you have no excuse!"[13]

Stephen's courage is indescribable. But his readiness to face the hell of the moment is even more unbelievable.

Imagine these religious hypocrites, decked out in their elaborate vestments, snarling at Stephen like dogs. What a scene they must have made as they dragged and pushed him outside the city limits, snatching up handfuls of rocks along the way.

Long before he was forced to face the trauma of the moment, Stephen had securely nailed down the nonnegotiables. Truth held him steady. He was ready.

And the importance of holding on to truth and being ready is not just for Bible characters.

Blow the Man Down

Who paid any attention to hurricanes? We certainly didn't.

In Pennsylvania, Chicago, central Texas, Indiana, and Middle Tennessee, the places where I had lived, the only time these giant pinwheel storms became topics of conversation was when they were catastrophic, like Camille in 1969, as she pummeled the Gulf, or Hugo's fury along the eastern seaboard in 1989, or Andrew in 1992, as he cleared out south Florida.

In January 2000, Bobbie and I moved to central Florida. And though we were moving to a state where hurricanes get personal, new friends and lifetime residents of our area were indifferent about them. Sure, there was the occasional tropical storm that whipped through on the tail of a coastal hurricane, taking out a tree or two, but living a full fifty miles from the ocean and almost seventy from the Gulf, we naively determined there was nothing to be concerned about.

Then one August morning, four and half years later, as I was slathering jelly on my early morning toast, the Weather Channel reported a category 3 (130 mph) hurricane named Charley was pounding Cuba. Once he finished with Cuba, the initial computer models had shown the storm taking a turn to the north, with Tampa and St. Petersburg in its crosshairs.

After passing over Cuba, Charley weakened slightly, dropping to a category 2 (110 mph). But in less than two hours, Charley took an abrupt turn to the northeast, gathering strength as a category 4 storm (150 mph), and headed for landfall in the Fort Myers area. The new computer model showed the hurricane heading straight up the Florida peninsula. Our home was directly in the storm's projected path.

I remember the sinking sensation. The gut-punching kind that makes the possibility of taking a deep breath temporarily undoable. You know the feeling, don't you?

But as that day unfolded, the sky was clear, the breeze "light and variable." A perfect Florida day. Neighborhood conversations revealed no anxiety at all. No dread or fear. In fact, the tone was almost celebratory. Adrian and Anna McCloskey, our wonderful Irish neighbors, spread the word that they were hosting a "hurricane party." Bring candles and a bottle of your favorite whatever. What could be more fun than riding out the storm with good friends?

The next afternoon, August 13, the refreshments were chilled, and a few candles were collected by the front door. We were ready.

A few hours later, around six o'clock, I was in my upstairs office, catching up on some e-mail. Weather.com was also on my computer screen as I tracked the storm. The early-morning dread I had felt the day before was completely gone. There was more anticipation than worry, just enough fear to make it exciting, like sitting on the front seat of a roller coaster just as it is reaching the pinnacle of the first steep hill and preparing to plunge.

Charley had come ashore at Cayo Costa, a small community north of Fort Myers, packing winds of 150 miles per hour. And he was moving rapidly northeast. The palm trees in front of our home took their familiar bows as the winds quickened. The rain picked up, waving across the street in sheet-like passes. Nothing unusual about this in central Florida.

I wonder what time we should head for the McCloskeys'. . . .

At about 8:30, something happened that I will never forget. The sound of the storm outside became angry and violent. Unlike the familiar sound of a hefty rainstorm, to which we were accustomed, this was something different, and I knew it. More like the timbre of a locomotive than the sound of a shower.

An explosion of wind and water blasted the front of our home. Our house trembled on impact. A band of tornadoes, which often ushers a hurricane across land, crashed into our neighborhood. Our two-story home groaned audibly, faced with winds unlike any she had known before. Water immediately seeped in from every south-facing window and door. A transformer, less than a block from our house, exploded. The lights went out. I raced to the linen closet and gathered up as many towels as my arms could hold.

I wasn't ready after all.

The McCloskeys' party—which, of course, never happened—didn't cross my mind until the next morning. We learned later that each of our neighbors had the identical experience when the tornadoes hit. No one showed up for the party.

As dawn broke, I walked the neighborhood to survey the destruction. Unable to stand against Charley's fury, large trees had tumbled into the street, a few onto their owners' homes. A big oak behind our house was one of the storm's casualties, barely missing our bedroom wall as it fell.

In a few hours, neighbors filled the sidewalks and streets. No one in our neighborhood owned a chainsaw, so cutting and chopping was done by hand. Folks who had never done more than nod or wave to the people down the street as they drove past were working and sweating side by side—cutting, bagging, sweeping. As cruel as Charley had been, the net effect of his windy swath was unfolding right here in our neighborhood. The ferocity unleashed on us had stripped away everything except what was most important to us: one another's safety. But this wasn't the last of the storms.

How Firm a Foundation

Less than two weeks later, weather experts spotted another major pinwheel headed our way. Unlike Charley, Frances was headed up the east side of Florida, predicted to make landfall at the town of Stuart. Computer models showed her traveling directly over our city once more.

We hadn't been prepared for Charley, but we would not be fooled again. In retrospect it's almost funny to recall the lines of people gathering material. Thousands of sheets of plywood were trucked to our area. Grocery-stores' shelves were cleared of bottled water and flashlight batteries.

Committed to doing whatever I could to save our remaining two large oak trees, I bought a dozen eight-foot two-by-fours to brace the trees against the storm.

Remembering what I had seen professionals do, I cut a few of the boards into sixteen-inch blocks and notched them to hold the braces. Then I banded the blocks to the trees with perforated steel strapping, connecting the head to the tail with a bolt. The final step was to set the boards against the blocks like a tripod.

Deciding that I needed to make one of the holes in the strapping larger to allow for the bolt that would hold it against the tree, I retrieved my power drill from the garage.

In my hurry I made a calamitous mistake. Instead of laying the steel strapping down on a block of wood, I held one end of the steel in my left hand, gently squeezed the trigger with my right hand, and began to drill. With the first few rotations, the drill bit jammed inside the hole I was trying to enlarge. Unexplainably, I didn't release the drill's trigger. Instead, I squeezed it to full speed.

In seconds, three feet of steel were pulled through my fist like a razor, wrapping themselves around the chuck of the drill like a sardine-can key. It was as if I had grasped the blade of a sword and someone had yanked it through my clenched left hand.

When the strap had finished its flight through my fist, I stood in horror, fully viewing the glistening white bones of two of my fingers.

"Oh, Jesus!" I hollered at the top of my lungs. "Lord Jesus! Lord Jesus! Lord Jesus!"

My friend Jerry Cummings, who had come by a few minutes earlier to see if I could use some help, ran into our house. With my blood spattered on his shoes, Jerry frantically went looking for Bobbie.

For Bobbie and me, the twenty-minute drive to Dr. George White's office was like one of the scenarios I mentioned at the opening of this chapter. With my hand wrapped around an ice bag and covered with a towel, this was one of those life-altering, hell-breaking-loose episodes.

Driving as fast as she could through Orlando's legendary traffic, Bobbie tearfully prayed aloud. She affirmed to the Father that we trusted Him in this horrific moment. She asked for special grace for me, regardless of the outcome. She even began to sing in soft, broken notes, the third verse of the hymn that had come to my mind the day baby Julie was born, thirty years before.

> Fear not, I am with you, O be not dismayed;
> For I am your God, and will still give you aid;
> I'll strengthen you, help you, and cause you to stand,
> Upheld by my righteous, omnipotent hand.[14]

In spite of Bobbie's amazing strength and encouragement, my body was trembling with shock. Remembering my grandfather, who had lost all the fingers of his left hand in a farming accident, my mind replayed nightmares I had experienced as a kid, fearing the same fate.

I was filled with uncertainty, moaning with dread as we drove east on Interstate 4 toward the surgeon's office. Laying my head back, I did my best to quiet my spirit and rest in God's providence and care. I tried to let the words from the hymn fill me with peace and assurance that God had heard Bobbie's prayer.

What have been your own defining moments like this? Times when something new in your wardrobe or driving the latest import or ascending the corporate ladder simply *did not matter?*

Times when it seemed that all hell had broken loose? For you?

These are the times when you and I need the rock-solid things that do not—and will not—change . . . before the wailing siren, before the surprise phone call, before the unexpected knock on the door, before the trauma at thirty-seven thousand feet or the ride to a doctor's office.

The Nailing-Down Part

Have you ever watched a carpenter drive a nail? It's quite a sight.

A guy who knows what he's doing with a hammer will rear back with his whole arm and, with marksman precision, crush the nail into the wood. Two or three blows and even a large nail is driven into place. Amateurs, like me, lift the hammer a few inches from the nail and gingerly tap it several times, doing their best to make a direct hit. Can you see the difference?

The final blow of the carpenter's hammer sets the nail—actually driving the head into the wood's surface. An expert will tell you that it's this strike that confirms the integrity of the nail's staying power.

At the end of each of the following chapters is a short section called "Setting the Nail." Here we will take one final look at what we've discussed. Then, like professional carpenters, we'll drive the "nail" deep into the surface of our minds.

Are you ready to start nailing? Here we go.

THE FIRST THING
TO HAVE NAILED DOWN:

God Is God: The Creator—Holy, Sovereign, and Merciful

What's the most important truth you'll ever hear? What would command every dimension of your life and thinking between now and the day you draw your last breath?

Until you and I have the following nailed down in our own thinking, the inevitable tragedies—the hell that breaks loose—will be our ruin. But if we do get this one thing nailed down, our purpose will be defined and our peace will be certain.

So, here it is . . . in a nutshell: God is God.

That's it. Pure. Simple. God is God.

In North America, giving assent to the existence of God is no big deal. For decades, polls have been taken, asking folks in shopping malls and on city sidewalks if they believe in God. Although the numbers shift slightly from poll to poll, the result is almost always a solid 90 percent yes. So you might think that it's an overstatement, the weight I'm giving to the supposition that God is God.

In other words, why would something that is so widely accepted be so profoundly important to nail down? With a 90 percent majority, don't we *already* have this first thing nailed down?

Let's save the answer for the end of this chapter.

God Is Great, God Is Good . . . God Is God

As a child, do you remember wondering about God? You probably did. I thought about God a lot as a youngster.

Attending church regularly, singing hymns, and listening to Sunday school lessons and sermons was certainly a major reason for this wonder. But there was more to it than those customary rituals. In fact, my next older brother, Ken, and I used to talk late into the night about God. "Just think . . ." our conversation would often begin. In the dark, from our bunk beds we'd talk about the preexistence of God.

"Just think," one of us would say, "God has always been. He had no beginning." And we'd lie there, silent in the darkness, and think about how God could be so big. So mysterious.

"Just think," the other would say, interrupting the stillness, "there's no end to space. It just goes and goes and goes . . . and never stops. And God made all of that."

And more silence.

In the years since the bunk-bed conversations, my childlike pursuit of God and the contemplation of His character have persisted.

I Am

Way back in the Old Testament, Moses had a "just think" bunk-bed conversation . . . with God Himself. The story of his life is very familiar: Pharaoh's daughter pulled his floating crib out of the Nile River; he grew up in the house of royalty. Later, the Israelites' release and crossing the Red Sea on dry land were added to his résumé.

But I believe the most significant moment in Moses' life came on the backside of the desert, a place called Horeb near the plains of Midian. Moses was tending sheep, minding his own business, when a bush on fire caught his attention. Actually, in the scorching heat, a burning bush was not unheard of. What was unprecedented about this particular flaming tumbleweed was that it had a voice . . . and it kept burning.

"Moses, Moses!" the voice from the unconsumed bush boomed.

"Here am I," Moses answered.

As Moses approached the flame, the voice spoke again. "Keep your distance," it warned. "And take off your sandals. The dirt you're standing on is holy."

"Who are you?" Moses asked.

"I am the God of your father—the God of Abraham, the God of Isaac, and the God of Jacob."[1] *Exodus 3:6*

Moses covered his face. Who could blame him?

In the conversation that ensued, God sent Moses on an impossible mission. He told him to return to Egypt, go directly to Pharaoh, and demand the release of the Israelites.

Of course, Moses resisted this assignment. Though the Pharaoh had known Moses from his infancy, Moses knew that making demands of someone so powerful could be fatal. *No one* told the Pharaoh what to do.

So Moses argued with the voice. "On whose authority am I demanding my people's release?"

"Tell them the God of your fathers has sent you," was the reply.

"What if they ask me your name?" said Moses.

And God said to Moses, "I AM WHO I AM."[2] *Exodus 3:14*

I Am . . . What?

When you and I meet someone for the first time, we often identify ourselves with someone else: "I'm her husband." "I'm his mother." "I'm her neighbor." "I'm his coworker."

When God identified Himself, He needed no modifier. Because He is completely independent, no one—no*thing*—was needed to finish the description. The subject and the verb were all that was necessary: "I AM."

The most basic foundation we stand on—the first thing we must have nailed down—is simply this: God *is* God.

He is present tense. He is right now. He is to be listened to—and reckoned with.

God Is Personal

end of at of sermon

Whoever you are, wherever you are, whatever you're doing, saying, or thinking . . . God is God. He is here. Right here. Right now. In this moment. Watching me. Watching you. Watching and listening.

Hundreds of years after Moses' burning-bush experience, the Old Testament king of Judah was facing the vast and overpowering armies of the Ethiopians. But in spite of overwhelming odds, God preserved His people and granted them victory. In summarizing the battle, the Bible announces God's watchfulness: "The eyes of the LORD search the whole earth in order to strengthen those whose hearts are fully committed to him."[3] *2 Chron. 16:9*

> *One of the evidences that God is God is the works of His hands. Simply look at what He has made.*

Just like the hidden cameras that keep tabs on us when we walk into a convenience store, God's attentive eye is trained on everything we do . . . including our thoughts.

This is the God who is *God*.

God Is God: The Creator

One of the evidences that God is God is the works of His hands. Simply look at what He has made.

The first ten words in the Bible give us the starting place: "In the beginning God created the heavens and the earth."[4] *Gen. 1:1*

What I love about these words is that God's creation speaks—shouts, actually—of the presence of a Master Planner in its design. The words are one thing; the results are their confirmation.

Let's Start with You

You were created by God, a marvelous display of His workmanship.

Regardless of who your parents are and the secret story of your conception, you are not an accident. Your birth was forecast from the beginning of time. Your body was intentionally and meticulously formed inside your mother's womb. Every cell; every blood vessel; every bone; every finger, toe, and organ came into being right on schedule and as planned . . . before the foundation of the earth.[5] And from the second you sucked in your first gulp of air to this moment, as you read these words, your internal organs have functioned without your help. (When was the last time you told your spleen to get busy?)

Eph. 1:4

The Orlando International Airport is our home airfield. Every year, more than 45 million visitors come to our area, and sometimes it looks like they're all standing in line at the same time. So, to save an hour or two when we fly out of Orlando, Bobbie and I bought "Clear Passes." To apply for these, we had to go through extensive security questionnaires and submit ourselves to thorough scrutiny. We also had our fingerprints recorded and the retinas of our eyes scanned. We passed inspection.

Now when we go to the airport, we walk past all those lined-up people—women, children, and grown men wearing black plastic mouse ears—and go straight to the "Clear" line. We either put our fingers on the reader or look into a screen. Our one-of-a-kind fingerprints and retinas match what they have on record, a little green light flashes, and we walk right through. We don't even need to show our passports or driver's licenses.

How is this possible?

Because in creating our amazing bodies, God gave us prints on our hands and retinas in the backs of our eyes that are utterly distinctive. No one who passes through our airport—or is living on the earth . . . or who has *ever* lived—possesses a match to your fingerprints or eyes. Your fingerprint, each retina, is one in multiple hundreds of billions. It's an overwhelming thing to consider.

Our physical bodies have whispered God's name since the moment we were conceived.

Every time you and I sit down to a meal, a miracle happens. We ingest leaves and meat and grains and milk and vegetables and bread and eggs and corn and French fries . . . all dead stuff . . . and God turns it into fuel. Without instructions from us, our systems—under His intentional direction—sort through all this matter and decide what's worth saving (the leaves) and what's not (the fries). In the silence, our organs pull nutrients out to keep us going and send the rest on its way.

The Bible says our bodies were created; the miracle of creation reveals this truth to us every day.

Looking Up

But it's not only the way our bodies were made and the way they work that whisper God's name. The creation outside our bodies does the same.

In the Psalms, King David said it perfectly: "The heavens declare the glory of God; the skies proclaim the work of his hands."[6]

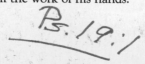

Ps. 19:1

The argument about how the worlds were formed has been raging for years. It will continue. Dr. John Lennox, distinguished professor of mathematics and philosophy at Oxford University in England, has said that the subliminal—and sometimes not-too-subliminal—mantra of the scientific world is this: "If you want a career in science, then you'd better give up the notion of God." As a Christ-follower, Dr. Lennox vigorously challenges that assertion.

For example, Dr. Quentin Smith, professor of philosophy at Western Michigan University, wrote, "Scientific theory that is confirmed by observational evidence tells us that the universe began without being caused. If you want to be a rational person and accept the results of rational inquiry into nature, then you must accept the fact that God did not cause the universe to exist. The universe exists uncaused."[7]

And Dr. Derik Parfit, distinguished professor of philosophy at New York University, once wrote, "No question is more sublime than why there is a Universe: why there is anything rather than nothing?"[8]

Dr. Parfit's question is completely appropriate. Why is there anything rather than nothing? The answer, I believe, runs directly counter to Dr. Smith's claim. The reason there is anything is that God determined that there should be, so He made the call.

"Let there be," God said, and there was.

"Okay, then prove it," an inquisitive student might say, laying charge of sourceless faith to my claim. Fair enough.

Scientists, by nature, are folks who spend sleepless nights conceiving and then confirming their theorems in laboratories. Historic proof, however, cannot be established this way. You and I cannot take historical assertions and re-create them in a lab to verify them.

If you told me that you went to dinner last night at one of your local favorites, and I challenged your story, you could not go to a laboratory and re-create the incident, settling the dispute once and for all. A historical event cannot be revisited and replayed. It happened, and time moved along.

However, you could look for ways to present evidence that would diminish my skepticism—an interview with your server, an eyewitness account from a friend who greeted you there, a neighbor who saw you pull out of your driveway at 6:15. The problem with historic "proof" is that you may never unequivocally remove my doubts. You may only be successful in swinging the pendulum from complete disbelief to a modicum of satisfaction.

"Okay," I might say. "I guess you *did* have dinner last night."

So how do we *prove* that Dr. Smith is incorrect? Can we take a bubbling beaker of something, pour it slowly into a test tube, and prove him wrong? How do we show him that the universe does *not* exist uncaused?

Let's take a look at two "evidences." These are my favorites.

Order

Even harder to believe than an uncreated universe is to believe that a randomly caused universe could have any order to it at all. Once created, who would instruct the heavenly bodies to stay in their orbits or hold steady in their galaxies?

The list of examples could be endless, but here's a simple one. Sometime today, log on to www.weather.com. Stroke in your zip code and it will show the weather forecast for you today. In the middle of the page you'll see the times posted for sunrise and sunset today, and sunrise tomorrow morning.

Question: How do the meteorologists know? Who told the earth to turn on its axis and to circle the sun at precisely the correct speeds so that sunrise and sunset—today and tomorrow—can be accurately predicted?

God ordered these things to happen, exactly as they do.

My conclusion, though it may sound cynical, is not cynical at all. I'm as sincere as I can be. Dr. Quentin Smith, too, is a man of profound faith and sincerity. But his belief in an "uncaused" universe denies the order and precision of a universe that gives plenty of evidence that it was created.

Here are a couple examples of created order:

- I don't know how cold the winter gets where you live, but no human being can survive more than thirty seconds if exposed to temperatures colder than seventy degrees below zero. Yet thousands of people are doing just that—this very minute—on pressurized commercial airliners. The earth's atmosphere is so carefully ordered that, unless we're traveling in a pressurized airplane, a simple voyage to a mere thirty-five thousand feet above its surface would quick-freeze us like instant-coffee crystals. Imagine how precisely we're placed on the earth's surface, comfortable in our surrounding temperatures but just a few miles from certain death.

- Our earth makes one complete spin every twenty-four hours. Since the earth is about twenty-five thousand miles around, at this instant, you and I are moving at more than one thousand miles an hour. But that's nothing. Since our planet encircles the sun once a year, we're also traveling at more than sixty-seven thousand miles an hour. A motorcycle cop would never have enough blank tickets in his pad. Once again, God's creation is so carefully ordered that, though we're moving at amazing and dangerous speeds, we're completely oblivious to any motion at all. To you and me, we are standing perfectly still, though our bodies are actually traveling along through space at thousands of miles an hour.

Oh, and one more thing about the order of our created universe: this isn't just about celestial bodies, or even our human bodies. The next time a fly lands on your picnic table, look carefully at its little body. Imagine how tiny the muscles that control its wings and legs must be. And think about how he sees with those compound eyes, each composed of up to four thousand individual lenses. In some ways, I can understand how grand things like the Tetons and Canyon are constructed and ordered, but a "simple" housefly? I don't think so.

One of the confirmations that God created the heavens and the earth is the order with which His work continues to operate. This would not be possible without a Creator.

Vastness

My second favorite piece of evidence for a created universe is its sheer size.

Let's have some fun with this. Let's pretend that you are able to let the air out of planet Earth, much as you could one of the tires on your car. So much air comes out that the entire earth is reduced to the size of a golf ball. Go ahead and pick up the golf-ball earth and turn it in your hand. Imagine our huge globe reduced to Titleist size!

Given this new reality, how far is your golf ball from the earth's moon? Just over four feet . . . about fifty-three inches.

And how far away is Mars?

More than two football fields away . . . about 634 feet.

And the sun?

A third of a mile.

And the distance to Proxima Centauri, the nearest star to the earth? Eighty-six thousand miles, almost three and a half times around our earth!

This is the vastness of our galaxy, but we're only scratching the surface.

Eta Carinae, another star in our galaxy, is so gigantic that if you hollowed it out, it could almost hold our entire solar system, from our sun to beyond the orbit of Jupiter.

And this star is only one of *billions* within our galaxy. The Milky Way—this oblong collection of stars—is so enormous that distance is measured by how far you would travel if you were moving at the speed of light: 186,000 miles a second. Going that fast, it would take you 1.2 seconds to get to the moon, 8.5 minutes to travel to the sun, and only 5 hours and 40 minutes to arrive safely at Pluto, the outermost heavenly body in our solar system.

But to make it across the breadth of the Milky Way would take you 100,000 years.

And now . . . take a deep breath . . . ours is not the only galaxy. The universe contains *billions* of galaxies just like our Milky Way.

How could you and I, in the farthest reaches of our finite minds, even conceive that all of this exists without a creator? Again, with all due respect, Dr. Quentin Smith is a man of outrageous faith if this is what he believes.

God Is God . . . He Is Holy

Do you remember when God asked Moses to take off his sandals because he was standing on "holy" ground? What, exactly, did that mean?

The word *holy* is found hundreds of times in the Bible. Its synonyms are many, but more times than not, it means "perfectly clean," "pure," "different," and "set apart."

Unfortunately, all of these synonyms are inadequate in actually defining God's holiness. God is different from anything or anyone we can imagine. He is unapproachable perfection.

Dr. James MacDonald says it this way: "God is more righteous and pure, more piercing and powerful, more strong and impenetrable than anything we can imagine. We comprehend only fractionally, even infinitesimally, all that He is. He's so different—so *other*—so holy. Every time you hear the word *holy*, think separation; He's completely apart and entirely different than you and me."[9]

God is meticulously independent, in a new category altogether. He is infinite and transcends anything we can understand.

The apostle Paul wrote to Timothy about God's nature: "He who is the blessed and only Potentate, the King of kings and Lord of lords, who alone has immortality, dwelling in unapproachable light, whom no man has seen or can see, to whom be honor and everlasting power."[10] *1 Tim. 6:15-16*

The great irony about God's holiness is that, though He lives in "unapproachable light," He draws us to Himself; no one has ever seen Him with the naked eye (John 1:18), and yet He invites us to come to Him as His children; He is a mystery, and yet He calls us to know Him. *us*

These counterbalancing truths have provided skeptics and cynics a vast playing field from time immemorial. Like the wind, God's holiness is indescribable except by virtue of what it does . . . the net effect of its unleashed impact.

When the Old Testament prophet Isaiah became aware that he was in the presence of a holy God, his response was not, "Oh, how *nice*. Hello, God." It was sheer terror. Because God's holiness was on display, the temple shook to its foundations.[11] *Is. 6:4-5*

After a hard day of preaching and teaching, one evening Jesus suggested to His disciples—seasoned boatmen—that they sail across the Sea of Galilee. So they did. But halfway through their voyage, they encountered a violent storm. So vicious was the wind that the boat began to sink.

> *Could it be that when all hell breaks loose, God is allowing the panic it creates to give us just a hint of His holiness?*

Waking Jesus from His nap back on the stern, the men looked on as He calmed the storm with the words "Peace, be still."[12] You and I might think that the disciples would have been high-fiving one another after what they had just seen. But they didn't. In fact, once they saw what Jesus had done and realized who He was, they were more terrified of being in His holy presence than of being hopelessly gripped in the jaws of the storm.[13]

In both of these accounts—the prophet in the temple and the disciples

Mark 4:35

in the storm—it was God's idea to show up. He was the one who turned Isaiah's world upside down, inspiring the fear that gobbled him up, the horror that transformed tough fishermen into whimpering children.

Could it be that when all hell breaks loose, God is allowing the panic it creates to give us just a hint of His holiness? Is it possible, when it feels as though our lives have run headlong into the pit of chaos and despair, that God is preparing us for His presence? *use*

In a Whisper

As inspiring as it is to talk about the power of the presence of a holy God, I suppose my favorite quality of His holiness is not seen in trembling temples or storms at sea, but in something even more remarkable.

Another Old Testament prophet, Elijah, was invited to walk to the top of a mountain to catch a glimpse of God's holiness: "And behold, the LORD passed by, and a great and strong wind tore into the mountains and broke the rocks in pieces before the LORD, but the LORD was *not* in the wind; and after the wind an earthquake, but the LORD was *not* in the earthquake; and after the earthquake a fire, but the LORD was *not* in the fire; and after the fire a still small voice."[14] *1 Kings 19:11-12*

Though its impact can be seen in building-shaking, earth-shattering, ear-splitting ways, God's holiness is sometimes as profound as a gentle nudge to our spirits, a tender moment of wonder when we sense His presence. God's holy companionship may come to us in the silent darkness of a sleepless night or in an uncharacteristic slice of solace while riding on a busy commuter train.

The lyrics of an old song unpacked the big compared to the small truth like this: "He's big enough to rule the mighty universe yet small enough to live within my heart."[15]

God is God, and He is holy.

God Is God . . . and He Is Sovereign

In our conversation about the order of the universe and the way food fuels our bodies, we have already touched on God's sovereignty.

Here is where we say good-bye to some scholars—those who consider themselves to be Deists. Because of the unmistakable harmony and vastness of creation, Deists agree that there was an "Intelligent Designer." They confirm a belief in God as revealed by nature and reason.

But once creation was completed, God went away, they contend. Not surprisingly, these people believe that the Bible is simply a document, conceived and written by men and women who did the work of writing it on their own. God's true "word" is not in print. God's word *is* creation itself, they say.

In this creation, say the Deists, it was God's plan to create mankind as caretakers of the universe, then to leave us alone. This deity has finished the work, and there is no longer anyone there with whom a "relationship" is possible or necessary. In retrospect only do we get to know the artist. We look back and study the artwork. Past tense.

I disagree with this claim.

Jumping Ahead

When I was a kid, our TV had three channels. Now there are hundreds, many of them 24/7 news stations. And all of these news channels have this in common: the format of open debate—folks sitting around a table and arguing. Sometimes the participants are open and civil. Sometimes they're combative and rude. To Bobbie's occasional annoyance, I admit to being a voracious consumer of these televised debates. Perhaps you watch them as well.

But after seeing many roundtable "conversations," I have never witnessed the following exchange.

Expert A: So those are my opinions and conclusions.

Expert B: Well done, my friend . . . and you know, I have never looked at the subject the way you've described it. I'm going to change my view. I apologize to the television audience for my previous, inaccurately stated position.

You haven't seen such a reversal either, have you? Instead, opposing sides hold their ground, often more upset (or enraged) at the end of the discussion than they were when the "on the air" lights went on.

I am a person of faith, a Christ-follower. But if you and I are on opposite sides of the debate on issues like God's activity in a contemporary world, I do not believe that I have the ability to change your mind. Only God can do that.

If you are a Deist (or a proponent of other free-thought philosophies), I would invite you to jump ahead to chapter 6, where we look at the "gift of faith." On the subject of the sovereignty of God and His continued activity in the universe, I believe that these things are only visible through the "eyes of faith."[16]

Faith is a "gift" to be received, because this is exactly how the Bible describes it.[17] No one can be argued or cajoled or pressured into faith. We can line up all the sound evidence and rationale for the Christian faith that can be uncovered, but a person can only believe in the truth of God's sovereignty when faith is present. Just as historical "proof" is ultimately inadequate in alleviating all doubt, no argument for Christianity is going to completely change a person's mind. That will only happen if—and when—they receive the gift of faith, the God-given ability to believe. Then they, too, can believe.

The person who has the gift of faith isn't smarter than the person who doesn't. He's just blessed. By definition, a gift is something that is not deserved and cannot be earned or intellectualized. The challenge to anyone who lacks faith is to simply dare to ask for the same gift.

What Difference Does God's Sovereignty Make?

Is the claim that God, as Creator, continues to be heavily invested in what goes on each day a conundrum, or a comfort? Is His sovereignty the logical reason given by people of faith when good things happen, and a rationalization when they don't?

In a sense, God's sovereignty is all of the above.

As order and vastness are confirmations of His creation, the sovereignty of God is simply the logical conclusion to His ongoing passion for what happens to what He has made. If a good parent wants to be involved in how well his children are doing when he sends them off to school, why wouldn't God want to do the same for His creation? His sovereignty covers everything . . . good and bad.

In all of recorded history, there may be no more graphic challenge to the sovereignty of God than the biblical account of the man named Job.

You and I could view Job's story as a random and natural sequence of events that God may have observed but in which He had no direct involvement. This view brings us to the inevitable conclusion that by pure chance, Job was one very, very unfortunate man.

In a single afternoon, the following things happened to Job: his cattle were stolen, his cattlemen murdered; fire dropped from heaven and burned up his sheep; his shepherds were also consumed; his camels were seized; the servants tending the camels were slain; and his house collapsed on his children, crushing them all.

If folks who win the lottery are considered "lucky," Job would be a powerball loser: one in tens of millions who turns up "unlucky." Job qualifies as the poster child for "all hell breaking loose."

But after careful examination, Job's story is the account of a man whose conclusion after his heartbreak and loss can be summarized in three words: God is sovereign.

Beginning with chapter 38 of the book of Job—after he, his wife, and his three friends have philosophized until they could philosophize no more about why these dreadful things had happened to him—God speaks. As the next four chapters unfold, God reveals to Job what He has done and what He continues to do. God begins His speech with reviews of His resplendent creation, the expanse of the celestial universe and the striking topography of the earth. Then God reviews His involvement in the wonders of the plant and animal world, including their marvelous procreation and daily survival and sustenance all in the present tense.

When God has finished, Job responds: "I know that You can do everything, and that no purpose of Yours can be withheld from You. . . . I have heard of You by the hearing of the ear, but now my eye sees You."[18] *Job 42:2-5*

Did you catch it? Job eventually nailed down the sovereignty of God when he gained a rightful look at the unimaginable brilliance of the Creator. Only after that could Job reap a clearer perspective of his own suffering.

There are only two alternatives—God's inability to be involved (or His mere apathy toward current events) or God's sovereignty.

When hell broke loose for Job, he gratefully chose to believe that God has knowledge of—and involvement in—everything that happened. He drew comfort from believing that nothing happens without God's permission.

Bone-rattling trauma of unexpected tragedy usually draws us toward God. As it was for Job, choosing belief in God's sovereignty over mere randomness brings the most comfort when our pain is most severe.

God Is God . . . He Is Merciful

Several years ago, the press published pictures of cleaning crews on location following a celebration of Earth Day. Truckloads of trash were rounded up after thousands of people gathered to pronounce their solidarity in the protection of a pristine Mother Earth. Though their intentions were noble, in honoring the earth, these celebrants couldn't help trashing her. Our natural bent is to *not* pick up after ourselves.

This propensity toward mess-making goes back a long time, and we have lots of company. Adam and Eve ruined their perfect relationship with God by disobeying, i.e., by making a mess. You and I have followed suit. Our predisposition to egocentrism, selfishness, greed, and unfaithfulness in relationships seems unavoidable. And the only way to rise above the mess is to get a clear picture of how a holy God sees us.

In the Old Testament, King David was the first to articulate the special way that God looks at our tragedies and failures by comparing the Lord to a dad.

> As a father has compassion on his children,
>
> so the LORD has compassion on those who fear him;
>
> for he knows how we are formed,
>
> he remembers that we are dust.[19]

And when King Solomon, David's son and the heir to the throne, prepared a sacrifice and prayed for the Lord to send a fire to consume it, all the people worshiped God, saying, "For He is good, for His mercy endures forever."[20] 2 Chron. 7:3

God is God; His presence is real. And God is the Creator, He is holy, and He is sovereign. But God is not a vindictive taskmaster or grade-school hall monitor looking to catch us in our humanity. As our heavenly Father, His benevolence toward you and me is legendary, and His kindness will last forever.

Even the best moments of warmth and security and affection and unconditional belonging that we ever experience in earthly families are only a shadowy glimpse of the compassionate, merciful love of God toward His children.

God's fatherly compassion was seen firsthand by the Old Testament prophet Jonah. Like a naughty older brother who wanted to hear his sibling scream from behind closed doors during a well-deserved spanking, Jonah witnessed the repentance of an entire city—one he would have preferred to see burn to the ground. So he sulked.

Jonah sat on a hillside and self-righteously grumbled, "You are a gracious and merciful God, slow to anger and abundant in lovingkindness."[21]

Unlike Jonah, the apostle Paul humbly speaks of the same merciful Father who saves us from His punishment. "But God, who is rich in mercy, because of His great love with which He loved us, even when we were dead in trespasses, made us alive together with Christ (by grace you have been saved)."[22]

For those who have attempted to distance their rational minds from a God who is, it's *this* attribute of mercy that sometimes changes their minds and opens their hearts to receive the gift of faith.

In describing the power of God's love, the apostle Paul wrote, "The love of Christ *compels* us."[23] The word *compels* literally means "to arrest." God's mercy is so profound, so powerful, so convincing and heart changing that once we have experienced it, resisting His love may be as futile as Jonah's attempt to out swim the big fish . . . or you and me standing on the seashore, trying to hold back the tide.

As hard as someone may try to argue with God's presence or His activity in the world, it may be His mercy that eventually settles the issue.

Setting the Nail

At the beginning of this chapter, you read that in most surveys, most people say they believe in God. You are I are in this group . . . so don't we *already* have this one nailed down? Not exactly.

The real difference between saying that we believe in God and nailing down the essential truth that God is God comes with knowing much more about this One in whom we believe. God is the Creator—this is what He has done; He is holy—this is who He is; He is sovereign—this is what He continues to do; He is merciful—this is how He treats you and me.

How many who say they believe in God would find their "belief" in Him adequate to sustain them when all hell breaks loose? Before it happens, it's essential that we have a solid and truthful understanding of who God is. God is God.

What you and I believe about God is the most important thing we will ever consider. Our beliefs will command every dimension of our lives and thinking between now and the day we take our final breaths. And when we're face to face with tragedy, knowing and trusting in a God who really is—and really is *here*—provides a certainty—a confidence in spite of the pain—that cannot be described.

The truth that God is the holy, sovereign, and merciful Creator is the central focus that will provide rock-solid perspective, comfort, and more hope than you can imagine.

See Page 46

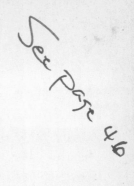

3

THE SECOND THING
TO HAVE NAILED DOWN:
The Bible Is God's Word

The Bible is accepted as one of the great literary masterpieces of world literature. From the crisp accounts of creation in its opening chapters to the stirring and picturesque apocalyptic visions at its close, the Bible tells the graphically human story of Israel's patriarchs, the Israelites' flight to Egypt, and their eventual settling in the promised land. Through poetry and gripping narrative, the Bible reveals the intricacies of the human condition, the oft-foretold story of the long-awaited Messiah, and the gruesome heartbreak of His execution . . . and glorious joy of His resurrection. The Bible uncovers the depths of mankind's fallenness and God's aggressive efforts in pursuing humanity with love and grace. The Bible includes the final outcome of history.

Most amazingly, the Bible claims to be the very *Word of God!*

But just a minute . . . I'm getting ahead of myself.

The Making of a Best Seller

I have spent most of my career in the book-publishing business. I'll admit that I didn't pay much attention to the publishing world until I was invited to join the staff of *Campus Life* magazine in January 1976. A few years later, Bobbie and I moved to Waco, Texas, where my publishing work changed from magazines to books.

Very soon after my job in Waco began, I got a picture of the simple goal that publishers have: turn skids of books in the warehouse into cash by making them best sellers. And in the decades that followed, I learned that there's nothing quite as exhilarating in this business as seeing a book you have published reach the lists that declare it a top seller.

One of the grim facts of the book business is that, for the average book, 48 percent of what it will sell over its lifetime will happen in the first ninety days after its release. In other words, the critical work of the publisher (and the book's author) is putting lots of capital and sweat equity into the book's *launch*—those first three months. Rarely will a book that crawled into the marketplace be swept up in an avalanche of sales in the weeks and months that follow. It either spikes up there . . . or it slowly fizzles.

Though this may sound a little obvious, one of the facts of the business is that when a book does catch fire and sell well, it happens because people are talking about it. In the business we say the book is "creating a buzz." And every time—*every* time—it's because of word-of-mouth advertising, one friend telling another how much he likes the book and what an impact it has had on him.

Until the early '90s, the best-selling book had sold 3.5 million copies. Recently, that barrier has been broken by several titles that have sold many more than a few million copies. One title, *The Purpose Driven Life* by Rick Warren (Grand Rapids: Zondervan, 2002), sold just under an unprecedented

30 million copies over a period of about five years. Unlike any nonfiction title in history, the buzz over this was unparalleled. People were talking, and books were selling.

But as remarkable as these numbers are, they don't come close to the annual sales of the Bible. Every year, year *after* year, more than 500 million copies of the Bible are sold or distributed. Since its first "commercial" printing on a Gutenberg press in 1455, more than 6 billion copies of the Bible, or portions of the Bible, have been distributed around the world.[1]

It would be impossible for a book—any book—to have sold so many copies if there wasn't plenty of word-of-mouth advertising and countless people being impacted by its message. It's not possible that all of these Bibles have been peddled under coercive pretense—"Buy this book and it will change your life . . . plus we'll throw in a vial of anointing oil and a prayer rug absolutely free."

And forget the typical book's product-life cycle—48 percent of its life-time sales within the first ninety days. The Bible is in a category all its own. Here's a book that has been available for mass distribution since 1455, and its sales have actually *increased* from decade to decade.

The inarguable fact of these numbers tells us something about the magnitude of the Bible.

The Bible? So What!

You and I have been looking at things that need to be nailed down before all hell breaks loose. We have talked about the essential need to understand and believe that God is God, that His presence is real . . . that He's right here, right now.

"Okay," you might say. "Now I know that when I'm facing an especially difficult time, I'm not alone. That's good. But why do I need the Bible? Isn't God enough without anything else? Not to mention that the Bible is so big and cumbersome. Isn't there a convenient little booklet I can just tuck into my pocket or purse that will be just as helpful?"

Let me answer these questions with an observation. Our belief in God—and our confidence in His presence, creation, holiness, sovereignty, and mercy—leads us to believe and trust the Bible as being His written Word. In the same way that *order* and *vastness* have helped us believe that a Creator fashioned our bodies, the universe, and the housefly, the veracity and reliability of the whole Bible leads us to the same kind of confidence in its authority.

Note

Though I'm only a businessman and not a theologian, I have had the privilege of opening the Bible week after week as a Sunday school teacher for over three decades. As a layman, I have also written several books that discuss the Bible and some of its themes.[2]

But my efforts and experience pale when compared to the work of people I know and trust who have received multiple graduate degrees and have taught the truth of the Bible at the seminary level or from a church pulpit for ages. These professionals follow in the train of multiplied thousands of Bible scholars and teachers down through the centuries, all of whom have drilled deep into the Bible and have found an endless supply of richness there . . . information, inspiration, and truth.

> *Trying to survive in a crisis—or in the daily grind of life—without the Bible is like being invited to a huge feast but going home hungry.*

Of course, God is enough. But why not go to the very supply that God has provided for us in the Bible—His Word? And why wouldn't we want to get to know God—and the way He deals with His creation—in a deeper way?

Trying to survive in a crisis—or in the daily grind of life—without the Bible is like being invited to a huge feast but going home hungry.

A Look at the Book Itself

As a publisher, an author, an editor, and a literary agent, one of the things that amazes me about the Bible is that the text—from Genesis to Revelation—was written by over forty-five writers over a period of fifteen hundred years. Can you imagine the potential for disagreement and error? One of the adages in book publishing is that a book with two authors is usually twice as difficult to finish as a book with only one. Imagine a book with forty-five!

And a single volume that wasn't completed for fifteen hundred years sounds like an impossible publishing venture, doesn't it? Imagine if America's founding fathers had started a book that still had over a thousand years to go before it was finished? We *can't* imagine it.

But this is the story of the Bible. And not only has it outsold all other published books in history, but its message is so profound that men and women have been willing to give their lives to defend it.

Don't let those words get past you too quickly. Who—or what—would you and I be willing to die for? When I was a kid, the threat of the Soviets kept those of us with vivid imaginations awake at night. Right along with fire drills in grade school, we had air raid exercises, anticipating the potential of a nuclear attack.

I'm really not sure how crawling under our little lift-top desks would have saved me or my classmates from anything, but somehow, tucked in a little ball on the floor, we felt better prepared for catastrophe.

In this context, we used to talk about our nation being invaded by Communists who would break into our homes and interrogate us about our beliefs, throwing us into concentration camps if we didn't recant our faith.

I so vividly remember wondering if I would have the guts to stand up to a life-threatening challenge like this. And I knew that down through the years, people had been cruelly put to death because they weren't willing to say that the Bible was merely a collection of men's thoughts and ideas, a book that was not singularly inspired by God.

The Story of William Tyndale

I was first introduced to William Tyndale as I turned the pages of *Foxe's Book of Martyrs* in the corner of my parents' living room. Of Tyndale, during his time as a student at Oxford University in the sixteenth century, John Foxe wrote, "His manners and conversation . . . were such that all they that knew him reputed him to be a man of most virtuous disposition, and a life unspotted."[3] I remember being impressed that Tyndale's buddies—those who knew him best—would say such noble things about him. I was also intrigued enough to read and reread the *way* they said it.

Later, as a student at Cambridge and a voracious reader of the Bible, Tyndale would often debate theological concepts with other students. But, Foxe tells us, his colleagues grew tired of his convictions and jealous of his relentless quoting of Scripture: "At length they waxed weary, and bare a secret grudge in their hearts against him."[4]

Under constant pressure from the local clergy, Tyndale quietly moved to London, where, for more than a year, he devoted himself to translating the New Testament into English, the "vulgar" language of the common man. Outspoken about his love for the Bible and his commitment to make the gospel available to all men, Tyndale continued the forbidden work with no concern for his own safety. Local clergymen, fearing that such common distribution of the Bible would put them out of work, forced him to leave England.[5]

So William Tyndale relocated to Germany. There he continued the tedious work of translating the Bible, including many Old Testament books. Though he was far from England, the English clergy continued to harass William, examining and mocking his translation.

Finally gaining the ear of the king to put an end to his work, Tyndale's enemies set a trap, using a fake dinner engagement with Tyndale's close friend, Henry Philips, as bait. Tyndale was captured and imprisoned in the dungeon at the castle of Vilvoorden for more than five hundred days. He was tried and convicted of heresy and treason.

In the early morning hours of October 6, 1536, the gentle William Tyndale was led into the prison courtyard. The executioner bound him to a large wooden post. Unwilling to beg forgiveness for having translated the Bible into English and recant his faith in Jesus Christ, Tyndale cried out, "Lord, open the king of England's eyes."

Just before setting fire to the kindling gathered around Tyndale's feet, the executioner strangled him until he was dead. In a few minutes, his body was consumed in the flames.

All of this for the unwavering belief in the power of a book . . . the Bible.

And Tyndale wasn't alone in his perilous defense of the Bible. Others were imprisoned, tortured, and assassinated because of their outspoken defense of God's Word. Patrick Hamilton was burned while kneeling at the stake; Henry Forest was suffocated in a dungeon rather than burned in a public place, because "the smoke of Patrick Hamilton had infected all those on whom it blew."[6]

Names of those who suffered and died in the Bible's defense include David Stratton, Norman Gourlay, Thomas Forret, and George Wishart—men who would allow neither fire nor sword to persuade them to disavow what they knew to be true about the Word.

Bringing It Home

A few evenings ago, Bobbie and I were walking our dog. We had just received the news that one of my college classmates and good friends, Christian

Stauffer, had died suddenly on a soccer field in Nairobi, Kenya. Chris and his wife, Hettie Hardin Stauffer, were schoolteachers on the mission field. Having spent an evening with Chris and Hettie in our home last summer, just before they left for their mission assignment, we were stunned by the news.

As we walked, Bobbie asked me if I was afraid of dying.

"No," I said. Then, stopping to think about our five grandchildren and how delighted I would be to watch them grow into young men and women, I added, "But I love living. I'm not eager to die."

It's hard to conceive that the same passion for life wasn't present in these heroes who died for the sake of the Bible. It was clear that they were not afraid to die. Though we have very little information about their families, we can assume that these believers were not eager to die. The martyrs must have had spouses and children or perhaps grandchildren that they loved very much, little ones whom they desperately wanted to watch grow up.

> They took the heat and held on to their beliefs when all hell was breaking loose for them.

These Christ followers willingly abandoned these dreams.

As I write about these who chose to die simply for the Bible—and the gospel of Jesus Christ that it contains—I'm stunned by their sacrifices. They made the choice, in fact, so that their children and grandchildren—and all who would follow, including you and me—would have free access to this priceless Book, in a language we understand. They took the heat and held on to their beliefs when all hell was breaking loose for them, so that when chaos and tragedy visits my home, I will have God's Word to comfort me—to give me God's perspective and a daily reminder of His grace.

Bobbie and I talked about the courage of these faith martyrs. "Just think of the sacrifice their whole families paid," she said.

The Bible, that Book you and I have standing like a quiet soldier on each of our bookshelves, has made its way into our homes, soaked in the blood of husbands, fathers, grandfathers, mothers, wives, grandmothers, and children . . . martyrs for the Book.

Another Matter of Faith

But how do we know the Bible is God's Word? As stunning as it is to read the stories of those who gave their lives for the Bible, how do we know that these people—and many others—weren't simply delusional, caught up in a frenzy of religious fervor? And how do we know that the Bible wasn't originally written and collected as a conspiracy to sway the thinking of these martyrs . . . and the vulnerable masses who listened to them?

As we discussed in the last chapter, historical proof, unlike scientific proof, cannot be unequivocally settled. And this is especially problematic since, in the pages that follow, I will use the Bible itself—as well as verifiable historical information—to confirm the Bible's veracity.

Harking back to some of the principles from my undergraduate class in logic, if a manuscript is filled with lies, why would any reasonable person use material from that *same manuscript* to determine whether or not it is filled with lies? That's a fair question.

This takes us back to the last chapter's discussion of the sovereignty of God and the pointed reference to faith.

No one has the skill to talk a skeptic out of his skepticism about the truth of the Bible. But through the eyes of faith, the Bible is a book that comes alive. By the power of God's Spirit, the words on the page become much more than mere words. They are God's voice—shouted or whispered, whichever is needed at the moment. These words are transforming.

A New Way of Seeing

Years ago, at nearly every shopping mall in America, there were kiosks that sold "magic eye prints." These computer-generated pictures were "magic" because as you stared at them, they slowly revealed three-dimensional images embedded within, images that you had not seen at first glance.

One afternoon, when we lived in Nashville, I was having lunch with a songwriter. As a child, he had received a black leather King James Bible from his grandmother. He remembered turning the fresh-smelling book over and over in his hands.

But soon the newness wore off, and the Bible was tucked in the back of a dresser drawer, then placed on a shelf in his closet, and finally packed away in a cardboard box. The songwriter told me how he had pursued a music career, complicated by addiction and abuse of every description. One bleak morning he awoke on a bare mattress in the middle of a strange room. No one else was in this room, or in the house. He had no idea where he was, where anyone else was, or why he was there. "It completely blew my mind," he recalled, the pain evident in his eyes.

"Shortly after that experience, something—perhaps Someone—nudged me and told me to look for that old Bible," he said. "But it was many months before I obeyed."

In the process of moving to Nashville, the songwriter found the cardboard box in his parents' attic. Sitting down on the dusty planked floor and in dim light, he opened the cover. There he read his own name and the inscription his grandmother had written. Chills ran down his body. Her warmth and kindness seemed to linger over the Book as he recalled his boyish excitement over the gift she had presented to him so many years before.

He began to turn the pages. As he did, he prayed, "Dear God, if there's something in here for me, please show me."

"It was just like one of those magic-eye prints down at the mall," he told me. "As if some of the words lifted from the pages, I saw things I had never seen before."

Drawn to know more, my songwriting friend soon decided to come to Sunday school. Carrying the same black leather King James Bible, he walked into our class and heard a passage being read from the apostle Paul's letter to the Ephesians: "But God, who is rich in mercy, for his great love wherewith he loved us, even when we were dead in sins, hath quickened us together with Christ, (by grace ye are saved)" (2:4–5 KJV). The King James English made perfect sense to him. He was reading the Bible using his own eyes of faith.

This is my hope for someone—maybe you—who may be uncertain about the Bible's truth. Certainly the Bible has been studied as great litera-ture for centuries. But the real test is the way God speaks to individuals through its inspired pages.

The History of the Bible

Though some of the Bible's authors are unknown, scholars have identified most of them—about forty-five in all. Beginning around 1400 BC, these authors began to pen the words that we now find in our Bibles. Their work was completed about one hundred years after the birth of Christ.

Unlike any other writings before or since, these texts were, according to their authors, written under God's special direction.

Because printing presses would not be invented for hundreds of years, multiple copies of these manuscripts were only possible as scribes duplicated them by hand, tediously rewriting each word and punctuation mark. A sec-ond, "attesting" scribe would read what had been written to verify its accuracy.[7] This kind of meticulous copying was employed for all ancient writings that were preserved and passed down, not just biblical manuscripts. But because their scribes were human, they experienced good days and bad. Their work wasn't perfect.[8] As you can imagine, this became especially problematic as copies were made of copies *of copies*, rather than from the original manuscripts.

So as we look at the reliability of any ancient work, naturally, one of the measures of accuracy is how old the copies are. How close to the original documents are they?

In his work *The New Testament Documents*, speaking of other ancient writings, Dr. F. F. Bruce tells us that the earliest copies of Caesar's *Gallic War* were found nine hundred years after it was written.[9] James MacDonald notes in *God Wrote a Book* that the earliest copies we have of Homer's *Iliad* were from four hundred years after its original writing.[10]

But of biblical manuscripts—again, completed around AD 100—the earliest existing copies are dated as early as AD 200, just a century after they were finished. We even have some fragments as early as AD 114, only a few decades from the date of the original.[11]

And how many of these copies do we have? Of Caesar's *Gallic War*, there are just *ten* copies; Homer's *Iliad*, about 650. But of the Bible, there are literally thousands: approximately 5,000 copies of the Old Testament and 10,000 of the New Testament.

And how did these manuscripts, written over a period of fifteen centuries, find their way into the single volume that we call the Bible?

One of the assignments of the third- and fourth-century church was to study many ancient writings, choosing which ones ought to be bound together in a single book called the Bible.[12] As they examined possible entries, they considered who the human author was and on whose authority the writer claimed to be writing. They also looked at the author's reputation and credibility, the content of the text, and its continuity with the other manuscripts.

But the most important qualification for a specific manuscript's inclusion in the Bible was the effect the reading of its text had on the lives of its readers. Were people more than just impressed with the work? Were they also impacted—even changed—by the power of the words?

The final, approved collection of the sixty-six manuscripts, or "books," is often referred to as the *Canon*, which simply means "measuring rod," the special criteria used to include certain works in the Bible.

What may be most amazing about the Bible—this collection of ancient manuscripts—is how it has survived multiple attempts to destroy it.

From the eighteenth-century Frenchman Voltaire to contemporary thinkers and writers, vigorous endeavors have been made not only to destroy physical copies of the Bible but to turn it into a mockery.

Much to the cynic's dismay, however, the Bible survives.

The contempt continues.

A student at almost any secular university right now will face some kind of opposition if he chooses to write a paper on the truth, reliability, *and* life-transforming power of the Bible.

Much to the cynic's dismay, however, the Bible survives.

But . . . in spite of its continued massive distribution, the Bible *still* could be an amazingly successful conspiracy of the most clever marketers and manipulators in history.

Or it could be the very Word of God.

Looking Ahead with Amazing Accuracy

Let's look at one more remarkable thing about the Bible.

You've probably noticed in early January that the checkout-counter magazine display at your favorite grocery store is usually full of magazines whose headlines boast of "New Year's Predictions." Some even call their forecasts "prophecies." Every once in a while, one or two of these guesses may even come true.

In the Old Testament, there are more than thirty-nine specific prophecies concerning the coming Messiah. Here are a few of them:

Messiah would be worshiped by shepherds:
"Those who dwell in the wilderness will bow before Him."[13]

Royalty would visit and lavish Him with gifts, including gold:
"The kings of Tarshish and of the isles will bring presents; the kings of Sheba and Seba will offer gifts. . . . And the gold of Sheba will be given to Him."[14]

Messiah would come as a baby boy:
"For unto us a Child is born, unto us a Son is given."[15]

Messiah's mother would be a virgin:
"Therefore the Lord Himself will give you a sign: Behold the virgin shall conceive and bear a Son, and shall call His name Immanuel."[16]

Messiah would be born in Bethlehem:
"But you, Bethlehem Ephrathah, though you are little among the thousands of Judah, yet out of you shall come forth to Me the One to be Ruler in Israel, whose goings forth are from of old, from everlasting."[17]

Amazingly, each of these predictions turned out to be true.

And What a Book It Is

The story is told of an American explorer who visits a remote, Pacific island jungle village. Amazingly, he finds a man in the village who speaks English. Even more remarkable is that the man is carrying a Bible.

"Oh, in America, we have outgrown that book," the explorer says, pointing to the Bible.

"Lucky for you, our tribe *hasn't* outgrown the book," responds the native. Then he adds, "Otherwise we'd be enjoying you for dinner tonight."

What *would* civilization look like without the influence of the Bible—if we were able to take a syringe and draw out its contributions to culture, the arts, education, medicine, business, and many other disciplines? Apart from telling the story of God and His activity among His people, the Bible—this ancient book—has provided us with a contemporary treasure trove. Here are a few examples.

The Bible defines marriage and intimacy: "Therefore a man shall leave his father and mother and be joined to his wife, and they shall become one flesh. And they were both naked, the man and his wife, and were not ashamed."[18]

Why should marriage be confined to a man and a woman? Why not *two* men or *two* women? Or one man and a dozen women? What about the man's sexual relationship with his wife? And what about the openness of their communication? How transparent should they be with each other?

The Bible is a manual on relationships. Reading it is like having your own personal counseling session each day.

The Bible prescribes right family relationships: "Submit to one another out of reverence for Christ. Wives, submit to your husbands as to the Lord. . . . Husbands, love your wives, just as Christ loved the church and gave himself up for her. . . . Children, obey your parents in the Lord, for this is right. Honor your father and mother. . . . Fathers, do not exasperate your children . . . bring them up in the training and instruction of the Lord."[19]

Like two gracious men reaching for the check at lunch—"I'll take it!" "No, I'll take it!" "Don't be ridiculous; it's my turn!"—here's how it works at home: *Husbands love and serve, wives honor and respect; husbands love and serve more, wives honor and respect more; husbands love and serve even more than before, wives honor and respect even more, and so on.*

Kids in these homes, listen to and obey their parents.

And dads should make reasonable demands on their kids. They shouldn't incessantly harp on them. Dads should tell their kids about God and their own love for Him.

Where are these practical instructions? They're in the Bible.

The Bible establishes the rules for labor and management: "Bondservants [employees], obey in all things your masters [supervisors] according to the flesh, not with eyeservice, as men-pleasers, but in sincerity of heart, fearing God. And whatever you do, do it heartily, as to the Lord and not to men. . . . Masters, give your bondservants what is just and fair, knowing that you also have a Master in heaven."[20]

Employees should do what they're asked, including working hard. And their work should be done with excellence. And why shouldn't bosses have the right to lord it over their employees, pushing them around like common chattel? Why should employers value their workers?

Because the Bible gives these relationships clear direction.

The Bible denounces discrimination: "If you really fulfill the royal law according to the Scripture, 'You shall love your neighbor as yourself,' you do well; but if you show partiality, you commit sin, and are convicted by the law as transgressors."[21]

Why can't I discriminate against women or children or against those whose ethnicity is different from my own? Because if I do, I'm sinning against God.

And how do I know how to value people?

It's in the Bible too.

Humanitarianism is a nonnegotiable: "Then the righteous will answer Him, saying, 'Lord, when did we see You hungry and feed You, or thirsty and give You drink? When did we see You a stranger and take You in, or naked and clothe You? Or when did we see You sick, or in prison, and come to You?' And the King will answer and say to them, 'Assuredly, I say to you, inasmuch as you did it to one of the least of these . . . you did it to Me.'"[22]

"Hey, listen, I'm busy," I might say. "I know there are folks around me who are needy—lonely, fearful, in pain—but I have a lot on my *own* plate. I'm just not naturally gifted at reaching out."

So why *isn't* it every man for himself? Why isn't it, in the words of Charles Darwin, "survival of the fittest"? What compels me to overextend myself, to step out of my comfort zone to serve? God's Word does. Because the Bible tells us that our service to the needy should be as high on our priority list as serving God Himself—He's tucked away right there in their struggle—and we must care for them.

The Bible addresses personal finances and stewardship: "I know what it is to be in need, and I know what it is to have plenty. I have learned the secret of being content in any and every situation, whether well fed or hungry, whether living in plenty or in want."[23] *Phil. 4:12*

When I'm tempted to buy something, I'm sometimes confronted with the thought, *Is this something I* need *or something I just* want? In the above verses, the apostle Paul challenges me by his own example to pursue contentment before I pursue anything else.

And check out these pearls of wisdom:

Whoever can be trusted with very little can also be trusted with much, and whoever is dishonest with very little will also be dishonest with much. So if you have not been trustworthy in handling worldly wealth, who will trust you with true riches? And if you have not been trustworthy with someone else's property, who will give you property of your own? No servant can serve two masters. Either he will hate the one and love the other, or he will be devoted to the one and despise the other. You cannot serve both God and Money.[24]

Money can be a cruel and very powerful ruler. Again the Bible slams this home when Paul writes, "The love of money is a root of all kinds of evil. Some people, eager for money, have wandered from the faith and pierced themselves with many griefs."[25]

Even circus magnate P. T. Barnum understood this biblical truth when he said, "[Money] is a very excellent servant but a terrible master."[26]

Imagine an ancient text that even tells how we should think about our money.

In addition to the things that are specifically articulated in Scripture, the Bible has also provided the inspiration that has launched incredible endeavors and institutions that we depend on each day.

Written communication: Around 1450, German printer Johannes Gutenburg was motivated to create a printing press with movable and interchangeable type so the Bible could be distributed more widely. In many remote parts of the world today, Christian missionaries are putting into written form those languages that had once been communicated only orally, translating the Bible in words that can be understood. This has given millions of the world's most neglected people a chance to learn.

Education: In early America, many public schools were organized to teach young children how to read and understand the Bible. Dr. Benjamin Rush (1745–1813), one of the signers of the Declaration of Independence, wrote, "My arguments in favor of the use of the Bible as a school book are founded . . . in the constitution of the human mind. . . . The memory . . . opens the minds of children. . . . Impress it with the great truths of Christianity, before it is pre-occupied with less interesting subjects."[27]

So pervasive was America's commitment to the Bible as foundational to education that, until the University of Pennsylvania was founded in 1751, every college and university in America was instituted to educate students in the truth of God's Word and to confirm the importance of a Christian worldview.[28]

Music, art, and literature: Visits to the great concert halls and art galleries of the world provide a loud testimony to the power of the Bible. German composer Johann Sebastian Bach initialed all his work with either "SDG," *Soli Deo Gloria,* "to God alone be glory," or "JJ," *Jesu juba,* "help me Jesus!" George Frederic Handel, Franz Joseph Haydn, Ludwig van Beethoven, Felix

Mendelssohn, Frédéric Chopin, Franz Liszt, and Johannes Brahms are among those whose life work was rooted in the Bible and in these composers' honor of God.

Artists like Rembrandt and Michelangelo used biblical themes, with passionate depictions of what they had read in the Bible.

And great writers, from Dante to Chaucer to Dickens to Tolstoy, Dostoyevsky, T. S. Eliot, C. S. Lewis, and J. R. R. Tolkien, were inspired by the Bible.

The power of God's Word stirred these great artists, musicians, and writers, not simply to collect material for their next composition, but to hear the voice of God. When you and I experience their work, our minds are touched by the same living Spirit that breathed beauty into their masterpieces, and our hearts are spontaneously lifted in wonder.

> *For centuries the Bible's compassionate message has inspired men and women to give their lives to bring healing to those in need.*

Medicine and hospitals: Though hospitals existed in antiquity—in Egypt, India, and the Far East—there is no doubt that the rise of Christianity in the first and second centuries sparked a deep-rooted connection between the Christian faith and health care. Today, medical missionaries number in the thousands. When disaster strikes anywhere in the world, many of the first responders to the hardest-hit regions are Christian-based mission organizations.

A visit to almost any city in the Western world puts a face on this truth. We see towering structures built to care for the sick, with names like Presbyterian/St. Luke's, Baptist Hospital, Saint Thomas, and Lutheran General.

For centuries the Bible's compassionate message has inspired men and women to give their lives to bring healing to those in need.

A Manual for Crisis in Your Life and Mine

During hurricane season, you've seen the reporters, decked out in slickers, standing in the pounding rain, getting pummeled by gale-force winds, and issuing warnings of an impending storm. Unwilling to heed their own advice, they say things like, "Do *not* go out in this storm. Stay inside your homes."

They also tell people who live in "low-lying areas" to head for higher ground. Dave Barry, my favorite humorist and fellow Florida resident, explains how easy it is to determine whether this warning is for you. "Go to your wallet and pull out your driver's license. If it says 'The State of Florida,' you live in a low-lying area."

Because Bobbie and I *do* live in Florida and have experienced a hurricane's devastation, we take instructions seriously. As a service to residents, the state provides us with plenty of emergency information that we can hear on local television or the Internet. When the wind outside is clocked at speeds in three figures, we will need help, and we know it.

The Bible provides the same kind of crisis assistance. When hell begins to break loose, its pages contain information we will need for survival.

As Moses' successor, Joshua knew something about staring down the gun barrel of danger. His task was to take the land that God had promised. All that stood in his way were armies that eclipsed the Israelites in might and numbers, not to mention the fortified cities that stood in strident defiance against any foe, especially an underequipped band of Jews. But Joshua knew exactly what to tell his people: "This Book of the Law shall not depart from your mouth, but you shall meditate in it day and night, that you may observe to do according to all that is written in it. For then you will make your way prosperous, and then you will have good success. Have I not commanded you? Be strong and of good courage; do not be afraid, nor be dismayed, for the LORD your God is with you wherever you go."[29]

A long time ago, the antidote for fear in the face of danger and the source for courage were found in a Book. They still are.

More Important Than Stockpiling Batteries and Fresh Drinking Water

In his letter to his young protégé, Timothy, the apostle Paul put a special emergency-preparedness lens on the Bible: "All Scripture is given by inspiration of God, and is profitable for doctrine, for reproof, for correction, for instruction in righteousness, that the man of God may be complete, thoroughly equipped for every good work."[30] Paul was saying to Timothy, "Here's what the Bible will do for you just when you need it. You may not even think of Scripture reading as preparation for all hell breaking loose, but when crisis *does* hit, you'll discover that getting ready is exactly what you've been doing. Here's what the Bible is good for—its special benefits." And here they are:

For doctrine: Have you watched a person taking the oath in a courtroom? He puts his left hand on the Bible and raises his right hand. The court clerk then asks, "Do you swear to tell the truth, the whole truth, and nothing but the truth, so help you God?"

Paul told Timothy that the Bible was profitable for doctrine. To create a good visual reminder of this, picture the courtroom witness with one hand on the Bible and the other in the air. The Bible *is* good for doctrine—"the truth, the whole truth, and nothing but the truth so help you God."

Whether it's for understanding of how the worlds were formed, for the account of human failure without God, or for the incredible story of redemption and grace, the Bible is truth—the one authoritative voice of absolute wisdom: "Then Jesus said to those Jews who believed Him, 'If you abide in My word, you are My disciples indeed. And you shall know the truth, and the truth shall make you free.'"[31] John 8:31-32

The Bible is without rival for teaching truth.

For reproof: When you and I are in trouble or away from God because of our own failure or defiance, we need reproof. This is God's way of getting our attention, like when you would hear your mom call you from the other end of the house as a child . . . and she would use your _whole name_. She was making sure you didn't miss the urgency of her voice.

Whatever it takes to get our attention, God will use it. In fact, sometimes the _benefit_ of all hell breaking loose is that it's precisely at these times that we hear God's voice most vividly.

> Sometimes the benefit _of all hell breaking loose is that it's precisely at these times that we hear God's voice most vividly._

In _The Problem of Pain_, C. S. Lewis reflects, "God whispers to us in our pleasures . . . but shouts in our pain."[32] And King David said, "The LORD is near to the _brokenhearted_ and saves those who are crushed in spirit."[33]

The Bible has a way of admonishing us and shouting hope that gives us the confidence to change.

For correction: Getting our attention is important, but it's only a setup for the news that is to follow. Once your mom had your attention, she probably made it clear what you had done to deserve this rousing interruption.

A truthful verdict is necessary for correction and change.

When you visit the doctor, do you want the truth about your condition? "Give it to me straight, Doc," you would say. A phony—or even diplomatic—representation of the diagnosis isn't going to be any help right now. It's not what you want.

In the chapters to come, we will look at what the Bible says about our condition. Some of the words might be painful, but a counterfeit diagnosis isn't going to get it. The Bible says, "Happy is the man whom God corrects; therefore do not despise the chastening of the Almighty. For He bruises, but He binds up; He wounds, but His hands make whole."[35]

God's Word corrects us.

For instruction in righteousness: The Bible is truth, helping us understand God's ways. It captures our notice and tells us where we've stepped out of line. Then the Bible lays out the plan.

For several years I had a boss who had a little wooden plaque on his desk. It read, "Don't bring me problems, bring me solutions."

A fitting subtitle under the words *Holy Bible* could read, "Go ahead and bring Me your problems; this book is filled with solutions."

King David boldly went before the Lord and gave us the very words to pray when we need help: "Cause me to hear Your lovingkindness in the morning, for in You do I trust; cause me to know the way in which I should walk, for I lift up my soul to You."[35] *Ps. 143:8*

"I will instruct you and teach you in the way you should go; I will guide you with My eye."[36] *Ps. 32:8*

The Bible lays out a plan to follow.

Setting the Nail

In 1995, a close friend called to tell me that Hollywood storyteller Jeffrey Katzenberg, one of the three principals at DreamWorks Animation SKG,[37] was looking for a "Christian consultant." Katzenberg and his colleagues had decided to put the story of Moses into an animated major motion picture, *The Prince of Egypt.*

Katzenberg's researchers had strongly advised him to find an advisor from each of the three world religions that embraced the story of Moses: Judaism, Islam, and Christianity.

After several phone calls and meetings, I was invited along with my friend and fellow believer Larry Ross, owner of a Dallas public relations firm, to be the consultant for the Christian viewpoint.

For nearly two years we met regularly with Jeffrey Katzenberg and his associates, inviting pastors and Christian leaders to meet at the Dreamworks studios to evaluate and discuss the movie script.

During one gathering, Jeffrey discussed with us how the vision for the movie was born. He told us of a meeting where Steven Spielberg, David Geffen, and he were discussing possibilities for their new studio's first major animated release. Because Jeffrey was the former Disney executive who had identified the story that later became *The Little Mermaid* as a candidate for great animation, Steven and David trusted his instinct.

"You're the great story picker," they jabbed. "What do *you* think?"

"Well, how about Moses?" Jeffrey responded.

They were at first taken by surprise that Katzenberg would select a story from the Bible. But soon they confirmed his choice. "Not bad," they said. "That story has been around for a long time. Let's do it."

As Jeffrey told our small gathering of Christian leaders this story, he became contemplative—a marked contrast to a man who takes intensity and drive to a whole new level.

"After my meeting with Spielberg and Geffen, I found a Bible and took it home," Jeffrey admitted. "I looked up the book of Exodus and began reading the story of Moses. When I was finished, I read it again. And then I read it again. And again."

He looked around the small room as we listened with rapt attention. When it dawned on him that we might jump to some conclusions about what he was telling us, he joked, "Now, don't get carried away. I didn't have a born-again experience or anything like that."

We laughed but still wanted him to go on and tell us exactly what did happen as he read the story from the book of Exodus.

"As I was reading the Bible," he continued, "something happened to me. Something I cannot quite explain. I knew that I had to retell this story, so I called my associates to tell them that we were going to tell the story of Moses for our first animated feature."

So began the process for DreamWorks' first feature-length animated film. For three years, six hundred animators drew almost 150,000 pictures, or "cells," depicting the life of Moses. In 1998, after an investment of nearly $80 million, *The Prince of Egypt* was released, earning well over $200 million worldwide.

Having seen *The Prince of Egypt* progress from storyboard drawings and partly composed songs, it was a thrill when Bobbie and I went to see the finished movie at our local theater. Reminded of Jeffrey Katzenberg's story of sitting down and reading the Bible, we marveled again at the power of the Scripture.

"It's amazing," was all we could say.

This book, this collection of ancient manuscripts, this best-selling book of all time that men, women, and children gave their lives to preserve. This book that still has the power to touch lives, to instruct, to convict, to be our comfort and our guide when all hell breaks loose . . .

. . . is God's Word.

USE THIS

THE THIRD THING
TO HAVE NAILED DOWN:
Mankind Is Eternally Lost and in Need of a Savior

It was not a pretty sight.

My friend James and I were in Atlanta. We had just finished one meeting and had allowed just the right amount of time—even *some* allowance for traffic—to get to our next one. In spite of our propensity toward adventure, we had even called ahead to make sure we knew how to get there.

"Turn north on Peachtree Industrial Boulevard," the receptionist told us, "and look for Sugarloaf Parkway. Our office is only ten or fifteen minutes from where you are."

I dutifully turned north. Though I did keep my eye out for Sugarloaf Parkway, I was also quite caught up in my conversation with James. The meeting we had just finished needed some serious debriefing . . . plus, since he lives in Chicago and I live in Florida, we had a little personal catching up to do.

Twenty minutes went by, then twenty-five, then thirty . . . and no Sugarloaf Parkway. "I thought this whole trip was only supposed to take ten or fifteen minutes," James finally said, glancing at his watch.

"Yeah, that's what I thought too," I responded, beginning to feel that sinking, "uh-oh" sensation in the pit of my stomach.

We called the receptionist again from my cell phone—frustrated and already a little late for our next meeting. The directions were repeated.

"Yes, we *did* turn north on Peachtree Industrial," I said, trying to hide the fact that the words were being squeezed through clenched teeth.

Then the receptionist asked me to tell her again where we had *started* our trip. I repeated our previous location.

There was silence on the other end of the phone . . . then a sigh . . . then, "Oh no."

The problem was that the location of our first meeting was *already* north of Sugarloaf Parkway. We should have turned south . . .

Suddenly I remembered that the whole time we had been traveling north on Peachtree, the southbound lanes were bumper to bumper—more like a two-lane parking lot than a highway. I had even pointed out the snarled traffic and commented to James about how glad I was that we weren't "in that nightmare."

Being lost is no fun at all. I know you've been there.

I turned our car around and squeezed into a space on the southbound lane of the Peachtree Industrial "Used Car Lot."

An hour later, we arrived at our meeting. What a waste. Of course, we joked with the receptionist when we finally arrived, but we were frustrated and it wasn't something we felt like laughing about.

Being lost is no fun at all. I know you've been there.

A Problem with the Starting Place

The interesting thing about my unexpected adventure with James was that we were in trouble the very first moment we hit the northbound lanes of Peachtree Industrial Parkway. Why? Because we had miscommunicated our exact starting point, and from that moment on, every mile we drove was a mile farther from where we wanted to be.

It's the same with you and me. In our quest to nail down the things we need to know before all hell breaks loose, we have to agree on our starting point.

Because of our human nature, the Bible says that we begin our journey lost: "Behold, I was brought forth in iniquity, and in sin my mother conceived me."[1]

Actually, it's worse than that . . . we're *eternally* lost. That's even more perilous than the Peachtree Industrial Used Car Lot.

And sometimes it's not easy to admit that we're spiritually lost.

Bobbie and I were attending a concert in the world-famous Ryman Auditorium in downtown Nashville. This auditorium, built in 1892 and funded by a riverboat captain, is considered by some to be the birthplace of country music.[2] It was intermission, and Bobbie and I were squeezing our way to the concession stand for some midcourse refreshments.

"Hello, Robert," I heard from a few feet away.

I turned to see someone I immediately recognized, a man who, along with his young family, attended our church. Bobbie and I had gotten to know Ray and his wife, Judy, several years before. They were regulars in our Sunday school class. We had even enjoyed a dinner party at their home with a handful of good friends. But as I looked at Ray now, it dawned on me that it had been several months since I had seen him at Sunday school . . . or at church.

I stepped out of line and shook Ray's hand. "It's good to see you, Ray," I said.

"Uh, it's good to see you too," he said sheepishly.

Then, like a sail snapping to attention with a welcomed puff of wind, Ray caught a breath of confidence. He seemed to remember something important.

"Judy and I stopped coming to church," he told me. "We've decided that it's best for our three kids not to go either."

I didn't speak. Instead, I did my best to communicate nonverbally to my friend that I welcomed his honesty and would be happy for an explanation, *if* he wanted to fill me in. He obliged right away.

"We just got tired of those prayers of confession that the minister has us recite during every worship service," Ray said, speaking with plenty of poise and self-assurance. "I don't like to hear that stuff about being a sinful person . . . my kids sure don't need to hear it either. It just doesn't build their self-esteem," he said with a marked edge.

Clearly, Ray was not looking for an argument—at least not right there in the lobby of the Ryman—with the second half of the performance about to begin. I searched for something to say, *something* that might draw Ray and his family back to church.

As we were about to walk away, I told Ray that Bobbie and I would love to see his family back in church and I was sorry that he felt that the prayer of confession was harmful.

We shook hands and said good-bye.

I watched as Ray walked away, turning north on Peachtree Industrial Parkway.

Every Minister and Teacher's Job Description

The inspiration for this "lost" thing came from my friend John Kramp, who wrote a book several years ago filled with some of the most creative and helpful ideas on telling people about Christ.[3] John introduced readers to "the laws of lostology." Lost folks, like James and me, blindly scooting north on Peachtree Industrial Parkway, are often unaware that they're lost.

John's book and Ray's problem with the prayer of confession forced me to take a careful look at how best to reach the people in our Sunday school class. In fact, it was the inspiration for my contacting Rev. Mark DeVries, our church's pastor to youth and their families.

In a few days, Mark and I sat down to talk. I told him about John's book and Ray, and how restless I felt. Mark confessed to some of the same thoughts, including a reevaluation of his call and his job description in pastoral ministry.

Before our brief meeting was over, we had concluded one critical thing about our job descriptions: there was nothing more important for us to make known from Scripture than the truth that we all are eternally lost and in need of a Savior.

But, like a passenger who dares to challenge the driver's sense of direction, we are at risk when we nudge folks—folks whom we love—toward recognizing that they are on the wrong road, headed nowhere. I suppose I'm feeling some apprehension right now . . . with you. Calling to your attention that the Bible says we are all eternally lost is probably not going to go down easily.

You and I, however, are in the *same* lost boat. Like my friend and I learned from our northward ride on Peachtree Industrial Parkway, we'd better have our starting point nailed down before we go any further.

What Is It About Our Hearts?

In Old Testament days, God called men to be prophets. Under their names on their business cards could have been the words "Thus says the Lord." Or maybe "Listen carefully, because what God has to say may make you miserable."

Take Jeremiah. His assignment, calling the people of Judah to repent, lasted almost fifty years. During that time he was threatened, tried for his life, put in stocks, forced to flee from the king, publicly humiliated by a false prophet, and thrown into a pit.[4] A man who never married, Jeremiah has often been referred to as "the weeping prophet." He took his job of telling people of their lostness very seriously.

"Cursed is the one who trusts in man, who depends on flesh for his strength," Jeremiah boldly said to his friends, passing along the words God told him to speak. "[Cursed is the one] whose heart turns away from the LORD."[5]

Then the prophet passes a gripping indictment on the heart of all people. "The heart is deceitful above all things, and desperately wicked."[6] Then Jeremiah adds, almost with a sigh of resignation, "Who can understand it?" Here Jeremiah is asking the question we can't get away from, the one you and I ask as well.

What *is* it about our hearts?

Eighteenth-century hymn writer Robert Robinson summarized the same idea about the lostness of our hearts prosaically when he wrote:

> Prone to wander, Lord, I feel it,
> Prone to leave the God I love.[7]

When our daughter Julie was a little girl, sometimes she would actually *try* to get lost when we were shopping. Not a victim of separation anxiety, even as a toddler, but a lover of hide-and-seek, she'd disappear behind clothing racks or curl up behind a counter, waiting until we'd panic and start calling for her. Her mother put an end to the unsafe game with stern warnings.

But, unlike Julie, you and I usually wander off more like the sheep in the New Testament Gospel of Luke, chapter 15. We nibble on a little tuft of grass here, then notice that the tuft over there looks better . . . then realize that the tuft *way over there* looks even better. "In no time," says Dr. James MacDonald, "we look around and ask ourselves, How in the world did I get over here?"[8]

Why do we wander from safety and get lost? Jeremiah told us. Our hearts are wicked . . . *desperately* wicked.

Although my friend Ray couldn't stand the words, they were still true: we *are* sinners. Like a plate of metal shavings exposed to a powerful magnet, without divine transformation our hearts are inexplicably drawn toward selfishness and pride and pettiness and gossip and avarice.

Someone might say, "Yes, but I know nice people who do lots of good deeds but have no time for spiritual things, and certainly no devotion to God." As beings created in God's image, we *do* have the capability of kindness and generosity and good deeds. Jeremiah didn't say that we don't have the tools to do these worthy things. What he did say—because God told him to—is that our hearts are in need of transformation, because they are deceitful and wicked. Our deeds may, on occasion, be exemplary, but our hearts need to be changed.

The apostle Paul says it another way, leaving no doubt that we're all in the same car headed in the wrong direction: "There is no one righteous, not even one; there is no one who understands, no one who seeks God."[9]

Here's the starting place for all of us: we must *know* that we need help. Like the hurricane party we scheduled at the McCloskeys' (but never had), lostness may sound like fun. But in the end, when all hell is breaking loose, it becomes a deadly nightmare.

None of my neighbors and I will forget how "partying and riding out the storm" actually sounded like fun. But two weeks later, when the next hurricane was on its way, coming toward us through Miami and southeast Florida, scheduling another party didn't even come up. In fact, getting ready was all we talked about. As the new storm was spinning our direction, I drove to Home Depot for plywood at five o'clock in the morning. All of our local home centers had advertised early hours for emergency supplies, but I figured that I'd be well ahead of the crowd.

In the darkness, I drove east on Conroy-Windermere Road toward the store. Not more than two miles from our home, the road crosses over the Florida Turnpike, the only major highway in Florida that goes northwest from Miami.

I gasped as I looked southeast along the Turnpike. Like a string of illuminated pearls, headlights formed a lighted chain that stretched as far as I could see. In the predawn hours, these cars, lined up bumper to bumper, were crawling northward. Floridians had been caught unprepared the first time. This time we knew better.

Accidents most often come without warning. We must be ready *in advance of* tragedy. Our understanding of our lostness should push us to get ready *before* all hell breaks loose. Any resistance to admitting our lostness is often just a result of pride.

The Peril of Pride

During the '70s, there was no defensive player more feared than the Oakland Raiders' Jack Tatum. After a few years in the National Football League, Jack earned the nickname the "Assassin." Get the picture?

Tatum was born and raised in New Jersey. And though he didn't play football until high school, it was soon clear to his coaches that he possessed enormous skills, along with an undeniable killer instinct, an especially useful tool for men who play football.

Jack was drafted by the Oakland Raiders, a team well known for its take-no-prisoners approach to the game.

On August 12, 1978, in a preseason game between the Raiders and the New England Patriots, a young, lanky wide receiver named Darryl Stingley was going out for a pass, a short "slant pattern" across the center of the field. Regrettably for him, this route took him into Jack Tatum's territory.

The pass from the Patriots' quarterback, Steve Grogan, sailed high and a little behind Darryl's outstretched arms. At the moment of Stingley's greatest vulnerability, Jack Tatum's helmet and shoulder crashed into the wide receiver's neck.

Darryl Stingley's body dropped to the turf like a stone.

The dreadful impact of Jack Tatum's high-speed tackle severed Darryl Stingley's spinal cord, rendering him a quadriplegic.

There was nothing illegal about the contact, and Jack Tatum knew it.[10] He stood for a moment over Stingley's lifeless form, lying facedown on the ground, and walked away.

Even three decades after the tragedy, Jack Tatum had reportedly never contacted Darryl Stingley. He did not call him in the hospital, and he never apologized or expressed any regret over the incident that rendered a brilliant ath-

> *I can fully identify the disdain of confessing my own errors.*

lete a motionless cripple. Not a single word. No expression of remorse for what happened that August day. No demonstration of humility or caring for ending a man's career.

Answering reporters who challenged his behavior, Tatum said he saw no need to apologize—because he hadn't broken a rule.

The peril of pride, pure and simple: an unwillingness to humbly express regret.

But before erecting a bronze statue of Jack Tatum in the town square as the town jerk, I am forced to take a careful look at myself. I can fully identify the disdain of confessing my own errors. Of course, my blunders may not appear as vicious as Jack Tatum's, but my propensity to pride and self-sufficiency can be profound. What about you?

That One in the Mirror

Greek mythology tells the story of a strikingly handsome young man named Narcissus, who fell on his knees one day, peered into a placid pond, and saw in the stillness his own image. At that moment, Narcissus fell deeply in love with himself.

In the New Testament, the same malady infected another young man. The Bible says that he was rich. He probably owned more things than the guy next door and therefore assumed certain things about himself—like how great *he* was. Whatever his assumptions, the man had "great possessions" and he took credit for them.[11]

One day the young man approached Jesus. The apostle Mark says that he "fell on his knees"—shades of Narcissus. His question actually sounded more like an attempt to pad his résumé than an honest examination of the Master.

"Good teacher," he said, shamelessly trying to flatter Jesus, "what must I do to inherit eternal life?"[12]

Here was a question that was unmistakably all about himself. "Since I'm such a big fan of myself," he may as well have said, "I want to live forever and enjoy *me* as long as I can."

"Have a big, free garage sale in the poorest neighborhood in town," Jesus told him, "and give all your stuff away."

The Master—since He could look directly into the young man's heart anyway—called his bluff and exposed the pride and greed living deep within. Jesus' words were more than the young man could take. He turned and walked away, his head down in defeat.

In late 1972, a youthful Carly Simon went to the recording studio and crooned a tune that instantly became the theme song for people who live with the world's narcissists. In January 1973, "You're So Vain" jumped to *Billboard*'s number one spot. The lyrics open with the account of a man wearing an apricot scarf and striding into a party, his hat "strategically dipped below one eye." The chorus rings out, "You're so vain, you probably think this song is about you . . . don't you, don't you?"[13]

But a prideful heart is nothing to sing about. In the book of Proverbs, King Solomon, a man who certainly was powerful, successful, and rich enough to deal with the temptations of pride, cuts to his own understanding of its dangers: "Pride goes before destruction, a haughty spirit before a fall."[14] Sounds like the voice of experience, doesn't it?

Before a devastating hurricane hits, pride says, "Hey, I can handle this. I'll just stay here and ride it out." After a man snaps his opponent's neck in a full-speed collision, pride denies breaking the rules and says, "It's not my fault." And like the wealthy young man, in the presence of God Himself, pride says, "I don't really care about the giver, but I sure would like more stuff."

Solomon says to every proud person, lost as he can be, "Change your attitude or you're going down."

Your Bootstraps Are Broken

"Pulling myself up by my own bootstraps" could be the motto of every proud, hard-driving, goal-oriented man or woman in the world. "He's a self-made man," for some, is the highest compliment a guy could ever receive. "Look what she's accomplished" is music to the ears of a determined, ambitious woman.

But when it comes to this issue of lostness, independence is a loser. You and I are not capable of making, finding, or saving ourselves.

Most of us who set New Year's resolutions can experience a *few* days or weeks of solid reform. But like the default screen on our computers, or wagon wheels that helplessly drop into the ruts on a muddy lane, we tend to fall back into old routines and habits. It's difficult *not* to.

Teaching through the Gospel of Luke in Sunday school several years ago provided a flashlight to see the real problem. After several months of studying the New Testament text, we had reached chapter 18. A few verses in, Dr. Luke illustrated the diagnosis with the words of Jesus. "To some who were confident of their own righteousness and looked down on everybody else, Jesus told this parable."[15]

Sounds like pride is not just a contemporary "illness."

Jesus went on to describe two men who had gone to the temple to pray. One, a Pharisee (probably with his turban strategically dipped below one eye) strode self-assuredly to the altar. "God," he began, "I thank you that I'm not like other men—robbers, evildoers, adulterers—or even like this tax collector," gesturing toward the man standing a short distance away. He went on to brag about the assorted religious rituals he practiced . . . uh, religiously.

At the same time, the tax collector—the target of the Pharisee's derision—bowed his head in humility. He even pounded his chest with his fists in contrition. "God," he prayed, "I'm throwing myself at your feet and counting on your great mercy. I'm a *sinner!*"[16]

Drawing the Sunday school lesson to a close, I concluded simply, "You and I are eternally lost and in need of a Savior . . . and we cannot save ourselves."

The next day, a man who identified himself as Chuck Willoughby called my office. He warned me that I probably didn't know who he was. He was right; I didn't recognize his name. He had been in class the day before and wanted to know if he could take me to lunch.

Quickly checking my calendar and happy to oblige, I said, "How's Thursday, 11:30?"

"That works," Chuck answered.

On Thursday, at the appointed time, a British-racing-green Porsche 928 pulled up in front of our building. It looked like something straight off the racetrack. My heart rate jumped to full speed. The passenger-side window lowered smoothly.

"Hi, I'm Chuck," said the friendly driver, leaning over far enough for me to see his face.

Opening the door and slipping onto the butter-supple leather seat, I shook Chuck's hand, fastened my shoulder harness, and off we drove to lunch.

"Nice car . . . *really* nice car," I said, making no attempt at any sort of cool-guy diplomacy.

"Thanks," Chuck responded. His warmth and sincerity were genuine. And even on the short drive to Pargo's, I could tell that, though he enjoyed his sophisticated car, he was not in love with it. I liked Chuck's easy manner and friendly disposition right away and remember thinking that this was going to be an enjoyable time.

Because it wasn't yet noon, the parking lot was practically empty. Chuck found a good spot close to the front door and whipped in, stopping on a dime at just the right moment. Even pulling into a parking space in a car like that felt good.

In a moment we were inside Pargo's.

"Table for two," Chuck said confidently to the hostess.

We followed her to the far corner of the restaurant, a perfect spot for a get-acquainted lunch.

Even before our waiter was back with our sweet tea, Chuck started talking. He told me that he and his wife Penny had not been regulars at church or Sunday school, but that his two growing sons had started to ask some difficult questions about life. "We thought they ought to be involved in a church somewhere, and we decided to tag along," he said.

Our drinks arrived, so we took a minute and ordered lunch. But as soon as our server turned to walk away, Chuck picked up right where he had left off.

"I was there last Sunday when you finished the lesson by saying that we are eternally lost and in need of a Savior and that we cannot save ourselves."

Chuck hesitated for just a moment and looked down and touched the condensation trickling down his glass of tea. Finally, he glanced up.

"I'm lost," Chuck stated, as directly and clearly as if he had been on a witness stand in a courtroom. "I'm lost," he repeated.

In the years since my first meeting with Chuck, I have reflected over the poignancy of that lunch. And Chuck and I have talked about it several times since. It was a life-defining moment: a man I had never known before, ten minutes into our first meeting, revealing an intimate snapshot of his soul.

As we enjoyed our lunch together, it was thrilling to assure him that a lost person can be found. How Jesus Christ died to save lost people . . . men like Robert and Chuck. Chuck's face radiated hope as he listened to how a person could confess his lostness—his sin—and receive the free gift of "foundness"—salvation. I encouraged Chuck to find a place to kneel down over the next few days and pray, expressing his heart to God in his own words.

After promising to think about all we had discussed, Chuck agreed to report back soon, then asked for the check.

Over the next ten years, almost everything in Chuck Willoughby's life changed. A string of events paved the way for a change of career. He left his lucrative corporate job and started a small video production company. A year later, I bumped into him at church. The transformation could only be described as remarkable.

"We're going to sell our house and make a big move," Chuck announced, an undeniable twinkle of certainty in his eye. "I'm going to seminary."

Today Chuck is a Presbyterian pastor and knows the joy of opening the Bible he loves and teaching his congregation about lostness and foundness. He and Penny are serving the Lord with enthusiasm and care and humility and distinction.

The last time I saw Chuck, he wasn't driving anything British-racing-green, but the radiance and joy of the man was visible . . . a man once lost and on his own, but now splendidly found.

No More Excuses

Sometimes lostness becomes a comfortable way of life. Like children looking around the playground for someone else who failed the test, we sometimes search for people who give us permission to stay lost and alleviate our guilt.

But when lost people are singled out and admit the truth, they can experience real change. A notable account in the Gospel of John sheds some light on this.

In the northeast corner of the wall that surrounded the city of Jerusalem, there was an opening called the Sheep Gate. Just inside this gate was a pool called Bethesda. Because there was no running water in homes, city engineers designed places where water collected so people could communally bathe and wash their clothes.

But there was something special about Bethesda. Occasionally the normally still water was, for some mysterious reason, stirred into a bubbly froth. Local residents believed that angels stirred the water, and when they did, the pool took on healing qualities. The first sick person to get in the pool after it had been supernaturally stirred would be miraculously healed.

There were five separate elevations around the pool—John refers to them as porches—where people could step into the water. Because of the healing power of the water when it was disturbed and the unpredictability of its occurrence, John tells us that a multitude of blind, lame, and paralyzed people gathered on the porches, hoping to be the first to climb into the trembling water and be healed.

Then John identifies one sick man—we're not told about his particular infirmity—who had dealt with his condition for thirty-eight years. Jesus approached him and asked him a pointed question.

Looking down at the man lying there, and knowing that he had been in that condition a long time, Jesus said to him, "Do you want to be made well?"[17]

What a question to ask a desperately sick person. At first glance, this sounds outrageous. It would have been logical—even appropriate—for the man to snap back at Jesus, "Duh! Are you serious? Do I want to be made well? I can't *wait* to get rid of this pain."

But this isn't how the infirmed man responded. The question Jesus asked revealed a deeper ailment than the physical malady that the man suffered.

"The sick man answered him, 'Sir, I have no man to put me into the pool when the water is stirred up; but while I am coming, another steps down before me.'"[18]

Did you catch what he said? Like a crafty politician in a news conference, the sick man sidestepped Jesus' question. He didn't say, "Yes, sir. I want to be healed." Instead, he revealed his belief that the situation was impossible to change. He whined about how difficult it was to get to the healing water.

> Like a crafty politician in a news conference, the sick man sidestepped Jesus' question.

One of the realities of a life of spiritual sickness—lostness—is that it can become our identity. Instead of having hope and receiving healing, sometimes it's easier for people who are lost to congeal with other lost folks and create a false sense of immediate relief.

It's like circling the wagons in the wilderness instead of looking for a way out!

The sick (lost) man at the pool of Bethesda had an identity. He was a sick (lost) man. Of course, no one had any expectations for him, given that fact. "Hey, that's the best he can do. What do you expect?" those people in his world—his family, his friends—probably said. "He's sick."

So Jesus' question meant something stunning to the man. *If I do get healed*, he might have thought, *everything in my life is going to have to change.*

What's interesting about the apostle John's telling of this story is the part he leaves out, because the next recorded words are from Jesus, who encourages the sick man to a new life.

"Rise, take up your bed and walk."

But what must have really happened between the sick man's excuse and the healing words he heard? His healing took place once he concluded that he needed to abandon this little sick-guy fraternity around the pool.

"Not only am I sick and in need of healing," the man might have said to Jesus, "but I'm sick of being sick. I'm ready to be healed, to step into life a well man. No more attempts to cover up by hiding among other lost people. No more excuses for me. Go ahead and call me 'found.'"

Please Help Me

Like every other boy in my junior high I tried out for the Franklin Tigers basketball team. Every few days the coach would post the list of names on his office door, telling us who should continue to show up for practice and, of course, by virtue of the fact that their names *weren't* on the list, those boys who needn't bother.

I made the first cut. Don't be too impressed; I think that first roster cut went from 250 eager seventh graders down to 200 survivors. After a few more days of tryouts, however, my name and my hopes dropped off the list.

For the rest of my life, I never made a school basketball team. I stopped trying after the eighth grade, for two reasons: (1) I was barely five feet tall, and (2) my dad preferred that I experience gainful employment.

Something good happened to me at age seventeen. I grew. In what seemed like no time, I was standing six feet, three inches tall. But I still never tried out for anything more organized than intramural basketball. (I say "tried out," but, of course, in intramurals, everyone gets to play.)

After college graduation, I was asked to join a YMCA league basketball team. My coworkers, who were organizing the team, saw my six-foot-three stature and drew a conclusion, a seriously inaccurate conclusion: he knows how to play basketball. The old adage warning not to judge a book by its cover could have been translated in athletic terms: "Never count on a teammate just because he's tall."

So there I was, wearing a real jersey with a real number (we used magic markers on old T-shirts in intramurals). A basketball player.

The problem was that it was all smoke and mirrors. Yes, I was tall enough to play the game and wear the jersey, but, no, I wasn't a player.

After a few games—and a few predictable performances—I began making excuses. "Boy, I just don't know what went wrong here," I'd gripe. "I guess I just had a bad day." Or the classic, "Could you believe that ref?"

One day, after plenty of frustrating and embarrassing court appearances, I made the painful confession to my teammates. "I'm not a basketball player," I said. "I've never made an organized team, and I don't really know what I'm doing out there."

They weren't surprised.

But since I had admitted my pathetic condition, I was free to ask them for help. There were some men on our team with years of college varsity experience. From then on, I would not be too proud to ask them for help. No more acting like I was playing below my skill level. With my confession, I was finally free to work on my game.

Like Chuck Willoughby and the man at the pool of Bethesda, when you and I admit that we're in trouble—lost and in need of radical help and can't help ourselves—then our healing is possible.

Without the phone call from the northbound lanes of the Peachtree Industrial Parkway, we'll continue to head off into our lostness, learning to deal with—anesthetize—the sinking feeling that comes from not knowing where we are or where we're going.

Setting the Nail

My siblings and I were sack-lunch kids. But although the stuff my mother put in those little brown paper bags was far more nutritious than the school lunches, there were times when brown-bagging it made me feel like a geek.

I remember coming into the kitchen early on school days and seeing my mother faithfully folding wax paper around the corners of turkey sandwiches—on whole wheat bread—and packing our lunches.

The interesting thing about packing a lunch is that it's done long before we're hungry for it. In fact, sometimes the stuff you're using in the preparation—mayonnaise, lettuce, cold slices of meat—seems incredibly unappetizing at the moment. But you know that a few hours later, when serious hunger strikes, this stuff will be delicious.

The truth about a full understanding of our lostness is that although things may be going along smoothly right now, hunger *will* strike, all hell will break loose. It's a certainty.

And the time to realize that our hearts are sinful is right now. And God knows our hearts.

When the winds have reached 100 miles an hour with wind gusts to 120 or 130, it will be too late to do anything about it. You'll just have to hunker down and take your chances. When the phone call comes and it feels as if someone has just kicked you in the stomach, will you know what to do?

Is truth nailed down, or does it seem as though everything is swirling out of control?

You may be a veteran lost person. A professional. You may be as good at this lostness thing as anyone you know. But maybe you're ready to answer a question that ought to have a familiar ring to it.

The water's bubbling. Are you ready to call out for help? *Do you want to be healed?*

THE FOURTH THING
TO HAVE NAILED DOWN:

Jesus Christ Died to Redeem Mankind

What are you going to do with Jesus?

Average folks don't walk around contemplating this question on a regular basis. Imagine finding your seat on a flight and properly stowing your briefcase under the seat in front of you. Then, turning to the person next door, you say, "Good morning. How are you?"

"Fine, thanks," he replies. "But I'm sitting here trying to decide what to do with Jesus."

Though no one may have ever said this to you on an airplane, what you and I do with Jesus carries more weight than we could ever imagine. This may sound a bit overstated, but it's not.

Someone Who Changed Everything

Let's pretend that this morning you stepped off a spaceship. Reading this book, it was the first time you had ever heard the account of the birth, life, death, and resurrection of the man named Jesus, and about His claim to be God's Son, the long-awaited Messiah.

Your questions to me would probably be predictable and fair. "Well," you would ask, "*was* He the One? Is He real?"

"Let's go for a drive," I suggest.

We jump in my car, and within three blocks of my house, we pass a building. "Here's a structure that was built in Jesus' honor," I say, pointing to a massive church. Out front is a huge cross.

"When was this built?" you ask, thinking that by some quirk of architectural stability, the edifice had been assembled soon after Jesus' life on earth was completed.

"Last year," I reply.

"Last *year?*"

We continue to drive. On our short trip around our town, you and I drive past no fewer than a hundred more buildings, constructed not only in Jesus' memory but for the purpose of honoring and worshiping His presence and activity in the *here* and *now*.

You're stunned at what's happened because of this little boy in Bethlehem. "How many of these building are there around your earth?" you ask.

"Well over a million," I reply. "From breathtaking cathedrals of stone and glass to hovels made of sticks and straw." You're speechless, but I'm not finished.

We drive back to my home and boot up my laptop. I log on to my favorite online bookstore and enter the keyword "Jesus." We discover that stroking in His name sends us to over a quarter of a million books *currently in print*, almost 270,000 of them.

"All these books about this boy?" you ask wistfully.

"Uh-huh."

We walk to my shelf and pull out my copy of *Foxe's Book of Martyrs*. For the next hour we read stories of men, women, and children who willingly walked to their own executions, simply to defend their right to claim Jesus—this little boy—as their Lord and Savior.

Then I show you my Bible and begin telling you how miraculously this book has been preserved—and how reliable the text is, even surviving centuries of pointed attempts to destroy it or mock its contents. I read some of the Old Testament stories, the prophecies foretelling specific facts about Jesus, and the detailed New Testament accounts of His birth, death, and resurrection. We read the story of how the church—all those buildings erected in His honor—got its start. And we read about how, someday, Jesus is coming back.

"After so many years, copies of this book must be very rare," you say.

"Not really," I respond. "Last year over a half a billion of them were distributed around the world, in almost every known language."

"Last *year?*"

"It's the best-selling book of all time," I add.

You shake your head in disbelief. The past few hours have stunned you. You sit in my home with plenty to ponder and very little to say.

"Was He the One?" you finally whisper.

I nod.

"He *must* have been." You pause, reviewing all that you've just experienced. "I believe in Jesus too," you finally say. "And, with all I have seen, I cannot imagine that there would be anyone on your planet who wouldn't believe in Him."

So . . . What Do You Think?

It may have been their first real vacation together. A planned getaway for Jesus and His twelve disciples was just what they needed after two years of ministering to the needs—body and soul—of throngs of people. No wonder they were looking for a break.

Many of the people around them were disabled and desperate. Daily down-and-dirty political battles with loudmouthed religious elites and the day-to-day rigors of walking from place to place were wearing as thin as their sandals. Not to mention the daily challenge of finding meals and accommodations for thirteen hungry men.

The place Jesus chose for their brief hiatus was perfect. The serene and lush Caesarea Philippi, located at the base of Mount Hermon, was about twenty-five miles north of the Sea of Galilee. This spot was so delightful that the Roman emperor Caesar Augustus had made it a personal gift to Herod the Great, the governor of that region.[1]

With this pristine setting as a backdrop for their brief retreat, Jesus and His disciples would have had time to rest, refresh themselves in the clear stream. There would be ample time for good conversation. It was here that Jesus asked the question that began this chapter, except He was asking it about *Himself*.

Actually, Jesus began with a less threatening approach: "What are folks out there saying about Me?"

You and I can envision the disciples looking at one another before anyone answered. *Where's He going with this?* they must have wondered.

"I've heard some say that you're one of the prophets come back to life," one of His comrades finally said. Several others nodded in agreement. "Yeah, like maybe Elijah," one commented. "Or Jeremiah or even John the Baptist," added another.

Though the Bible doesn't give us much detail about the conversation, there may have been a wisp of silence following the exchange. And in the quiet, perhaps the men intuitively knew that Jesus' next question wouldn't be as easy to answer as the first one.

Their expectations were correct.

"And who do *you* say that I am?" Jesus asked, looking into each face in His own penetrating way.

I wish He hadn't asked that, they must have thought.

Jesus was not speaking to the multitudes. He wasn't addressing His question to the Pharisees, the appointed gatekeepers of Messianic inquiries. No, Jesus was asking His closest friends, men who knew Him as intimately as a two-year road trip could have afforded.

Simon Peter spoke up. Like a class full of students happy to see someone else volunteer an answer, the other disciples must have heaved a collective sigh of relief.

"You are the Christ—the Messiah—the Son of the living God," rolled off Simon Peter's tongue, almost as effortlessly as if he had been reading the words from a script. That's exactly what he was doing. Jesus immediately gave God the Father credit for Peter's declaration.

"Well done, Simon son of Jonah," the Master said. "No man could have said that unless God had told him exactly what to say."[2]

What bewilders me is that, after two years of hanging out together, the *disciples* didn't answer Jesus' question *in unison*. There isn't even a record of a cumulative affirmation from the others, nothing that says, "And the other disciples agreed." Even after two solid years of watching, listening, and experiencing the person of Jesus, didn't these men have the courage to step up to the question with a confident response?

No wonder "What are you going to do with Jesus?" is a tough question to answer.

Not a big fan of mass marketing, Jesus concluded the dialogue by asking—telling—His closest friends to keep a lid on it: "Then He commanded His disciples that they should tell no one that He was Jesus the Christ."[3]

Theologians and scholars have wrestled with the "why" of Jesus' refusal to flamboyantly pronounce His messiahship. Any reputable advertising agency or public relations firm would have certainly recommended a more aggressive approach. If Jesus *had* signed a contract with an agency that knew how to exploit an announcement like this, He could have created a worldwide buzz.

But Jesus knew that the fame spawned by such publicity would radically change His game plan. So He did His best to keep to truth of His deity under wraps.

There would come a time later in Jesus' ministry for full disclosure. Timing was everything. For example, near the beginning of His ministry, Jesus the Messiah entreated the healed leper, "See that you say nothing to anyone [else]."[4] Instead, "the [leper] left there, [and] he began to . . . spread the news about Jesus. As a result, Jesus could not enter a town if people saw him [or heard that He was coming]. He stayed in places where nobody lived, but people came to him from everywhere."[5]

> *Since we're lost, we need Someone trustworthy who knows how to find us. Jesus is exactly who we're looking for.*

Such are the perils of fame that Jesus desperately tried to avoid.

What are you going to do with Jesus? is not to be shouted to grandstands filled with sports enthusiasts or from the stage of a concert hall jammed with screaming fans. It was a simple question posed to Jesus' circle of friends. A question asked of you and me in the quietness of our hearts.

And before all hell breaks loose for us, we'd better have the answer firmly nailed down. While dodging traffic on a frantic ride to the hospital, nothing could be more dreadful than to not know who Jesus is or what we're going to do with Him.

Since we're lost, we need Someone trustworthy who knows how to find us. Jesus is exactly who we're looking for.

What Did Jesus Say About Himself?

In spite of Jesus' attempts to sidestep the spotlight, there were times when direct questions regarding His identity were inevitable. Not long after His private holiday with the disciples, there was the encounter in the temple at Jerusalem. And this time, a question was asked of Jesus concerning Himself.

"And Jesus walked in[to] the temple, in Solomon's porch. Then the Jews surrounded Him, and said to Him, 'How long do You keep us in doubt? If You are the Christ [the Messiah], tell us plainly.'"[6]

The same question that had bewildered the twelve disciples a few weeks earlier confronted the theologians of the day.

It's likely these same disciples were in the temple with Jesus when the Jews confronted Him with "If You are the Christ, tell us plainly."

Like an experienced witness facing an attorney's crafty interrogation, Jesus reminded these Jews that His works—miracles—should have confirmed to them that He was the Christ. But because they didn't belong to Him—His accusation infuriated them—they still didn't get it. Jesus finished His comments with a statement these folks didn't want to hear: "I and My Father are one."[7]

In case you wonder if these men took this claim—that Jesus was equal to God—casually, they didn't. Instead, they picked up stones and threatened to execute Jesus on the spot. Again, because of God's timing, He was able to escape.

I Am the Way

Not long after the confrontation with the Jewish leaders came the festival of the Passover.

On Thursday night—the evening of Judas's betrayal—in the setting of the Upper Room, Jesus told His friends who He really was. And once the awful events of the next few days were past, He said they would be strong enough to follow Him.

With the same authority He had displayed under the cynical scrutiny of the pompous Jews, Jesus told His friends: "I am the way, the truth, and the life." He said, "No one comes to the Father except through Me."[8]

Throwing Down the Gauntlet

Jesus' comments about Himself in the temple and the Upper Room change everything. His words remove Him from the ranks of history's "good men." Because of Jesus' claim to be more, no longer do scholars have the right to consign Jesus to the category of "great religious figure" or "moral teacher" or even "prophet."

In the last chapter we looked at the brief exchange between Jesus and the wealthy young businessman. Remember how the man bent down on his knees and addressed Jesus as "good Teacher"?

Jesus' question in return was simple and direct: "Why do you call Me good? No one is good but One, that is, God."[9]

As it turned out, because the rich man wasn't willing to believe that Jesus was God, his opening greeting was nullified.

"You can't call Me good and not believe that I'm God," Jesus was saying. Jesus had thrown down the gauntlet.[10]

Jesus' words seem brusque, don't they? "C'mon," some would say. "Give the young man credit for getting it partially right. Doesn't he score *some* points for recognizing Jesus as 'good'?" Isn't it better to say that Jesus was "good" than to say something negative about Him?

Actually, no.

Is God Just My Copilot?

Robert L. Scott had always wanted to be a fighter pilot. But when the world was suddenly thrust into the throes of World War II, he got stuck flying transport planes into China. But one day, Scott got his chance, eventually persuading his general to let him fly with the courageous band of aviators known as the Flying Tigers. While in this squadron, Scott engaged in combat with the deadly Japanese pilot known as Tokyo Joe.

In 1945, Warner Bros. released a film based on Scott's story. The title, *God Is My Co-Pilot*, though an admirable-sounding assertion, is bad theology. If Jesus is good, then He's God . . . because He *said* He is. And if He's God, then you want Him at the *controls*, not in the copilot's seat. If He's not God, then you're better off flying solo.

You and I do not want a liar as our first officer. His selection as our "copilot" would be a reckless one.

C. S. Lewis frames this truth in his inimitable, straightforward way: "You can shut [Jesus] up for a fool, you can spit at Him and kill Him as a demon; or you can fall at His feet and call Him Lord and God. But let us not come up with any patronising nonsense about His being a great human teacher. He has not left that open to us. He did not intend to."[11]

When all hell breaks loose, you and I do not want Jesus riding shotgun. He needs to be at the wheel. No one who makes false claims to be God ought to be our navigator, our nurse, or our go-to guy when things go badly. Consigning our desperation to such a fraudulent person would be foolish.

It's easy to follow this logic, but let's be honest. Even if we believe Him to be who He says He is, submitting ourselves to His control is no small assignment. Again, C. S. Lewis says it so well: "The terrible thing, the almost impossible thing, is to hand over your whole self—all your wishes and precautions—to Christ."[12]

Of course, he's right.

In the chapters that follow, we'll find out what "handing over your whole self" and putting Jesus "at the wheel" actually look like, but for now, let's get the truth about Jesus' identity nailed down and see what He accomplished for us. And since our beliefs affect our behavior, it's essential to have the facts firmly in place before all hell breaks loose. If we wait, it'll be too late.

Perfect Timing

Are you impatient? When you're sitting at an intersection and the light turns green—after it was red for what felt like an hour—and the driver in front of you just sits there, chatting on his cell phone, what do you do?

When you choose the grocery checkout line that's the shortest, but the person in front of you tries to pay his bill with a check from the First National Bank of Neptune, and the clerk has to call the manager, who's cleaning up a chemical spill back in housewares, what do you do?

Don't be too hard on yourself. You're in good company. The Jews were also impatient folks, and their wait was not about something as trivial as these common distractions.

When you go to a theatrical production, the curtain closes between scenes. This gives the director and stage hands time to rearrange the set for the next act. This happened in the historical drama of God's chosen people—between the close of the Old Testament and the beginning of the events of the New Testament. But, unlike the few minutes you wait at a play—or at the intersection, or in the grocery checkout line—this curtain was closed for four hundred years.

Two centuries before the close of the Old Testament's chronology, Israel's homeland had been split and conquered. The people were taken as exiles to Babylon. Under Nehemiah and Ezra's leadership, many captive Israelites had returned to the promised land to rebuild their homeland. But having lived in a pagan Babylonian culture for seventy years had a predictable result. When they returned home, many of God's people had forgotten Him.

Prophets stood before the people, declaring God's judgment and their nation's desperate need for a Savior. Some people repented. Most did not.

And then all communication from God and His appointed messengers went quiet. Four centuries and the curtain did not move. God was silent.

Unfortunately for those who had found their way back to Canaan, opportunistic warriors had their eye on this land. Alexander the Great conquered Palestine (the name given to Israel during that time), soaking the people in Greek culture. In fact, Alexander conquered lands in order to do one thing: change the way people thought. In doing this, he tried to abolish the idea of "God is God." Because the Greeks had co-opted the pagan gods of Egypt, Asia Minor, and Persia, their religion was come-one-come-all—the more gods, the merrier.[13] Alexander embraced the worship of multiple gods and lived to promulgate it throughout the world.

Those Jews who had faithfully worshiped the one, true God must have felt devastated when they saw everything they believed torn to pieces?

But during the four-hundred-year silence, the pummeling of the Jews was not only philosophical; it was also geographical. Like a baton in a relay race, the Jews and their land changed hands multiple times.

One of the conquerors was Antiochus III—"Antiochus the Insane." The Hitler of the second century BC, he sacrificed a pig on the sacred altar in the temple and ordered immediate execution of anyone caught with even a small portion of holy Scripture. Just as William Tyndale would do two thousand years later, some refused to relinquish their precious texts, choosing death instead.

After Rome conquered Palestine, Herod the Great was appointed king over the Jews. So despicable was Herod that he ordered the firstborn of every family to be killed on the day of his own death so there would be plenty of mourning. He knew that the day he died would otherwise be met with celebration.

So for four hundred years the Jews, waiting in silence, had taken a literal pounding on every front. They were ready for a Savior.

The Curtain Goes up, and God Speaks

After four centuries of sovereign quiet, God compassionately lifted His voice.

A New Testament scripture summarizes the moment:

God, who at various times and in various ways spoke in time past to the fathers by the prophets, has in these last days spoken to us by His Son, whom He has appointed heir of all things, through whom also He made the worlds; who being the brightness of His glory and the express image of His person, and upholding all things by the word of His power, when He had by Himself purged our sins, sat down at the right hand of the Majesty on high, having become so much better than the angels, as He has by inheritance obtained a more excellent name than they.[14] *Heb. 1:1-4*

One very long sentence in the book of Hebrews reveals what happened when the curtain went up. But despite the sentence's length, don't miss the message.

An exercise that always baffled me as a grade-school kid was sentence diagramming. Our teacher, Mrs. Sands, would draw a horizontal line on the chalkboard and challenge us to look at a sentence and determine the subject, the verb, and, if there was one, the object. Diagramming this one sentence from Hebrews could have taken a whole school afternoon.

> *God broke His silence by sending one last prophet—a shaggy and brash one—to announce that Jesus was on His way.*

If you haven't forgotten how to parse a sentence, let's take a shot at this massive one.

The subject is God. The verb, *has spoken*. Okay, that wasn't so difficult. Your fourth grade teacher would be proud.

For these Jews, sitting on the edge of their seats, the wait was worth it. Finally God had broken the silence. After four hundred years, God spoke.

And what did He say?

God said . . . "Jesus."

If it had been up to you and me, the strategy God used to break the seemingly interminable silence would probably have been a slick marketing campaign. But, consistent with Jesus' unorthodox methodology of declaring His messiahship, God broke His silence by sending one last prophet—a shaggy and brash one—to announce that Jesus was on His way.

He could have scrawled the news of the coming Messiah on the side of a blimp and floated it over Jerusalem—He had all the necessary technology, even back then—but He didn't. He sent a prophet named John the Baptist instead. And the long-awaited message delivered by John wasn't, "Hey, great news! The Messiah is on His way, and He's going to put an end to your bondage and persecution. Just sit back and He'll rescue you."

Instead, he told everyone, including the most pious among his listeners, to get ready by repenting. It wasn't exactly what they wanted to hear, especially since *they* were the ones who had been victimized.

But John was unrelenting. "You brood of snakes," he said. "Prove by the way you live that you have really turned from your sins and turned to God. Don't just say, 'We're safe—we're the descendents of Abraham.' That proves nothing. God can change these stones into children of Abraham."[15] **MATT 3:7-9**

What utter frustration for these Jews. Instead of a liberator to overthrow their captors, they faced a wild man as outspoken as the previous prophets.

"Don't tear your clothing in grief," the Old Testament prophet Joel had said four hundred years before. "Instead tear your hearts. . . . Return to the LORD your God."[16] **Joel 2:13**

John the Baptist delivered a message that was rough and confrontational. No attempt at diplomacy here. "[The Messiah] will baptize you with the Holy Spirit and with fire. He is ready to separate the chaff from the grain with his winnowing fork. Then he will clean up the threshing area, storing the grain in his barn but burning the chaff with never-ending fire."[17] **MATT 3:11-12**

Then Jesus arrived. And once again, the public relations campaign was awful. A baby boy was conceived in the womb of a young, single woman, understandably raising the eyebrows of even the most liberated Jews in Nazareth. Nine months later, the "illegitimate" son was born in a stable on the outskirts of the tiny hamlet of Bethlehem. Not counting the animals, the only witnesses to the birth were His mother, His adopted father, and a handful of shepherds and angels.

Why did God introduce His Son without a more effective approach? Let's go back to that long and powerful sentence in Hebrews for the answer:

God, who at various times and in various ways spoke in time past to the fathers . . .

It helps to review the drama from the opening scene. The first "act" was creation; the second was God's call to Abraham and the Old Covenant promise of the Jewish nation. Now it was time for act three: the Messiah— the New Covenant—and the liberation of God's people.

. . . has in these last days . . .

At the time of the writing of the book of Hebrews, Jesus had ascended back to heaven. Just before disappearing into the clouds above His stunned disciples, He promised that He would come again. The period between His ascension and His promised return—the days we're living in right now— are referred to in the New Testament as "the last days." This is the fourth act in God's drama.

> If we want to know what God has to say, we can hear Him plainly. We simply listen to Jesus.

. . . spoken to us by His Son . . .

God was speaking. In a way that can only be defined as mystery, from the moment of Jesus' birth and for the thirty-three years that followed, God the Son slipped into a head-to-toe outfit of human skin and sinew.

As heaven's resident for all eternity past, God's Son had never known physical pain, hunger, thirst, winter's chill, summer's heat, exhaustion, or poverty. On earth, He would experience all of these in His human nature, starting with His birth in a cattle trough.

From the moment He first uttered words, when Jesus spoke, His voice was God's voice. God said, "Jesus," and Jesus said, "I and My Father are one."[18]

John 10:30

If we want to know what God has to say, we can hear Him plainly. We simply listen to Jesus.

. . . whom [God] has appointed heir of all things . . .

Jesus was God's only Child, His only begotten Son (John 3:16). There is nothing that belongs to God that doesn't also belong to His Son.

When my grandpa Wolgemuth—"Father Wolgemuth" to nearly everyone who knew him—died, the family divided his meager belongings: his books, some memorabilia, and the tools from his workshop. After his clothes were given to charity, his car was sold and the money put in a trust along with the proceeds already there from the sale of his farm several years before.

All the important papers and documents of his life, including those granting full access to his trust, were emptied from the desk in his study and placed in a single cardboard box. That box was given to my dad. As an only child and sole heir, the contents of this box were completely his.

In His hands, Jesus Christ holds all things . . . and it's a lot more than a bunch of papers, checkbooks, deeds, and other stuff in a single cardboard box.

"For it pleased the Father," the apostle Paul wrote, "that in [Jesus] all the fullness should dwell."[19] *Col. 1:19*

. . . through whom also He made the worlds . . .

The baby Jesus is celebrated at Christmas. But don't let the infant confine your celebration merely to the holiday season. God's Son has existed before all creation. In fact, creation was His doing: "All things were made [by Jesus Christ], and without Him nothing was made that was made."[20] *John 1:3*

Here's the single most powerful biblical passage that unpacks Jesus' identity. "[Jesus Christ] is the image of the invisible God, the firstborn over all creation. For by Him all things were created that are in heaven and that are on earth, visible and invisible, whether thrones or dominions or principalities or powers. All things were created through Him and for Him."[21] *Col. 1:15-16*

The very star that guided the wise men to the Christ child had been fashioned and hung in place *by that same baby*. The truth of His identity and deity is astonishing.

. . . who being the brightness of [God's] glory . . .

In the Old Testament, God is revealed as a jealous God. Yes, He's compassionate and long-suffering, but despite His gracious nature, there's something He's not willing to share: His singular perfection and glory.

The second commandment delivered to Moses on Sinai says it plainly: "You shall not make for yourself a carved image—any likeness of anything that is in heaven above, or that is in the earth beneath, or that is in the water under the earth; you shall not bow down to them nor serve them. For I, the LORD your God, am a jealous God."[22] *Ex. 20: 4-5*

As our daughter Julie says, "God isn't a big fan of idols—anything that tries to take His place." As a young mother, she knows the importance of guarding her affections. God is not willing to share His glory with anything or anyone except His Son.

One of the most memorable stories of God's glory in the Bible is recorded right before the second set of stone tablets is inscribed.[23] Moses naively asks God if he can take a peek at His countenance. *Ex. 33: 18-22*

"You cannot see My face and live," God tells Moses. "But if you'll tuck yourself between a couple of great big rocks, I'll pass by and give you a glimpse of My back."

So overwhelming was the slightest glimpse of God's glory that the residual effect on Moses rendered him as radiant as a full moon on a clear night. The next time Aaron and the Israelites saw Moses, "the skin of his face shone, and they were afraid to come near him."[24] *Ex. 34: 30*

The writer addressing the Jews in the book of Hebrews announces that God not only *shares* His glory with His Son, Jesus, but He boldly proclaims that Jesus *is* God's glory, the most dazzling part of the brightest thing known to man.

JESUS CHRIST DIED TO REDEEM MANKIND

We cannot comprehend that glory with our finite minds, just like kids who are told not to stare at the sun or it will burn their eyes.

. . . and the express image of His person . . .

Although there's no way to thoroughly describe how God and Jesus share the same glory, we do understand the idea of a copy, or a duplicate image. For several years, I worked in the darkroom of a commercial photographer. Placing a negative into the glass carriage of a printer, the negative's image was projected onto special photographic paper. The paper was then sent through a sequence of chemicals, which created a photograph— a print. To produce another print, I'd put another piece of paper beneath the projected image and run it through the same chemicals. Because these pictures came from the very same source, the two prints were *exactly* alike.

Jesus is God, an exact likeness of the original. When you've seen one, you've seen the other. Since in our humanity we're not able to see God, He sent a duplicate to earth in plain view for all to see.

. . . and upholding all things by the word of His power . . .

When we talked about the sovereignty of God, we mentioned the Deists—those who believe that God created all things, then took the rest of eternity off and left creation to function without Him. But contrary to this belief that God went on vacation, Jesus, God's exact image, *is upholding* all things by the word of His power. This is in the present tense. Last night's sunset and this morning's sunrise happened because Jesus Christ ordered the earth to rotate our neighborhood away from and back into the sun's glow at just the right times. If He hadn't, we either would have been frozen in darkness or burned up in light.

. . . when He had by Himself purged our sins . . .

In 2004, Australian actor Mel Gibson produced the major motion picture *The Passion of the Christ*. The movie chronicles the final hours of Jesus' life prior to His crucifixion. It would be safe to say that this movie sparked a boatload of controversy and misunderstanding.

In the *New Republic*, Leon Wieseltier called the film "a repulsive, masochistic fantasy, a sacred snuff film."[25] Andy Rooney, the *60 Minutes* editorialist, called Gibson "a real nut case."[26]

In some ways, these critics are right. God's eternal strategy regarding the death, burial, and resurrection of Jesus *is* incomprehensible. It has been controversial and misunderstood since it first happened. It *is* vile and repulsive: "He [was] despised and rejected by men, a Man of sorrows and acquainted with grief. And we hid, as it were, our faces from Him."[27]

Gibson, like the rest of us who believe, can be taken for a fool.

Even the apostle Paul admitted, "For it seems to me that God has put us apostles on display at the end of the procession, like men condemned to die in the arena. We have been made a spectacle to the whole universe, to angels as well as to men. We are fools for Christ."[28]

What Jesus endured was a heinous display. And believing in Him puts us in the company of those who have been maligned for centuries. But the story is true.

Look carefully at these words: "When He had *by Himself* purged our sins."[29]

This is one of the most important things you will ever hear about the celebration called Easter. To satisfy the demands of a holy God, Jesus sent *Himself* to die. It was the only solution to the conundrum of God's love for us, and the sinfulness—lostness—of our hearts that kept us from Him.

Once Jesus had finished His gruesome—yet redemptive—task of taking our sin upon Himself, His dead body was placed in a cave on a Friday afternoon. Sunday morning, Jesus' body took a breath. Then another. And another. He opened His eyes and slowly sat up, removing the linens that had shrouded His lifeless body.

He stood and walked out of the cave alive.

. . . *sat down at the right hand of the Majesty on high* . . .

God's incarnate Son, Jesus Christ, showed up on earth as a commoner. But now He's back in heaven, where He belongs. His surroundings are no longer the Judean hills or the Galilean sea; they are the royal accoutrements of a throne room more regal than you and I could ever imagine.

And some day, He is coming back to earth, just as He promised. When He does, we'll shield our faces as Paul did on the Damascus road. The brightness of Jesus' glory will shine with radiance beyond comprehension.

Follow Me

Simon and his brother, Andrew, were fishing—doing what they did for a living. Walking along the shoreline, Jesus called to them, "Follow Me."

Matthew was minding his tax-collecting business. Passing by, Jesus said to him, "Follow Me."

With each of the twelve disciples, who left their lives behind and followed Him, Jesus' summons was simple and straightforward.

The invitation is the same for you and me. Jesus, God's Son, calls us to follow Him. So we follow because He is worthy to lead, to take charge. To be in complete control.

"In the Event of an Emergency"

There are six words you hear every time you fly on an airplane: in the event of an emergency. Only those passengers who've never flown before or have nothing to read are paying any attention.

But if our plane was actually headed in a downward spiral and about to crash into the ocean, we *would* listen to the instructions about our life vests and the inflatable rafts stowed away, wouldn't we?

The Weather Channel is interesting to watch. Sure, I'm curious about the predicted conditions for my golf game on Thursday and how cold it's going to be in Chicago or Charlotte, where members of my family live.

But when a hurricane is making a direct hit where I live in Florida, I listen to what the experts say as intently as if my life depended on it, because it does.

When Jesus invited twelve ordinary men to follow Him, life for them was ordinary and uneventful. Is the same true for you?

But what about the day when the wheels come off, when all hell breaks loose?

Because we're lost and need directions, Jesus says, "Follow Me."

Right now.

"Come to me," the Savior says, "all you who are weary and burdened, and I will give you rest"[30]

Setting the Nail

My nephew, Erik, and I were sitting at Jacobs Field, directly behind the Cleveland Indians dugout. During the fourth inning my pager went off, the piercing tone plainly audible in the middle of a noisy ballpark.

I looked down to see who had called. The display read, "143-47."

"143-47," I said out loud. "What's that?"

Erik looked at me, his bright blue eyes wide with delight. "My dad," he said. "It's my dad."

God speaks "I love you" in a way that leaves no doubt.

"What?" I said.

"Yeah, it's my dad, and he's saying he loves me." Then, amid the clamor of a Major League Baseball game, he explained. "My dad made up this code," he said. "It matches words with numbers. There's one letter in *I*, four letters in *love*, and three letters in *you*: 1-4-3."

"What's the four-seven?" I asked, completely taken with Erik's enthusiasm.

"That's how old my dad is," he laughed. "He's forty-seven, so I know the message is from him."

God also sent a message—a code—that we could understand. He knew that if He stretched skin onto Himself and visited earth in human form, He would be speaking a code that you and I clearly understood.

God spoke. He spoke "I love you" in a way that left no doubt.

God said, "Jesus."

6

THE FIFTH THING
TO HAVE NAILED DOWN:

Grace and Faith Are Gifts

Though decades have passed, we still look back on it with delight . . . "Bicycle Christmas."

In 1982, our family lived in Waco, Texas. Missy was eleven, and Julie was eight. Until then, the girls' bicycles had been hand-me-downs from friends or bargains from a neighborhood garage sale—basic, unpretentious transportation. Though some of their friends sported spiffier rides, our girls didn't complain. As far as we could tell, new bikes were not on their radar.

As the holidays approached that year, Bobbie and I talked about investing in brand-new bicycles for the girls. We had made a secret visit to a local sporting goods store on our way home from a date-night dinner and had tentatively picked out bikes we thought they'd really like. I remember envisioning how much fun it would be to completely surprise them on Christmas morning.

I took some blankets to the bike shop so we could pack the shiny treasures in our trunk without scratches, and we bought the bicycles—*and* matching bike locks. Then we called our neighbors, Stan and Linda, to see if they'd let us store them for a couple weeks in an empty corner of their garage, with an old sheet thrown on top.

The days leading up to the big day crawled by. It was hard for me to think about anything else. I even asked our neighbors if I could look in on the bikes. They understood. I wanted to do it twice but didn't have the courage.

During those days, when I'd pull my car into our garage and see the girls' rusty bikes, I'd smile, knowing that their days were numbered.

Finally, Christmas morning arrived. I had retrieved the booty from Stan and Linda's the night before, hiding the bikes away in our guest room. Bobbie and I had decided that we would wrap up the bike locks and give them to the girls as their last present. Then, while they were unwrapping the locks, I'd sneak away to the guest room and wheel the bikes into the living room.

When the time came, the execution of our plan went like clockwork. The gala of gift opening was finished, except for the two last presents. We handed the girls the wrapped bike locks, and I slipped out. When they looked up, there I stood with two new bicycles. Of course, they hollered and squealed with delight. There was a lot of jumping up and down.

Kneeling down, with tears streaming down *my* face, I hugged them both as they bounded across the room into my arms. Then they ran to hug and thank their mother.

There's nothing quite as exhilarating as giving something very special to someone you really love. You probably have a memory just as magical stored away.

God's Two Gifts ·

God has two incredible gifts waiting for you and me. There's no need for hiding them in the neighbor's garage for safekeeping; there's not a chance of spoiling the surprise.

The First Gift. The story of God's visitation to earth in Jesus Christ is an amazing one. Sending *Himself* as the only way to satisfy His anger over sin *is* the greatest story ever told. You may have heard this truth referred to as His "gift of grace."

"Thanks be to God," the apostle Paul wrote concerning Jesus, "for His indescribable gift!"[1] 2 Cor. 9:15

We're going to talk about this gift of grace in more detail later, but there's nothing we have done or can do to earn God's grace gift. We are given the gift of Jesus simply because He loves us. Though our lives seem rusty and broken and we wish we could make them better, it's only through God's mercy and grace that brand new lives are possible.

Again, the apostle Paul leaves no doubt about how this gift came to be. "When the kindness and love of God our Savior appeared, he saved us, not because of righteous things we had done, but because of his mercy."[2] Titus 3:4-5

Admittedly, parental love is only a shadow of the love of God, but His grace resembles Bicycle Christmas. Our kids had not done anything to earn their gifts. They didn't even know that new bikes were waiting for them at Stan and Linda's house. Bobbie and I had simply decided to give them the bicycles. All the girls had to do on Christmas morning was take what we had provided for them.

> *You and I do not have the capacity— the understanding— to receive God's grace.*

So it is with God's grace. He gives it to us, and we receive it. Simple enough.

But there's something we need to know about receiving this unmerited gift of grace. It's something that may completely surprise you, but it's true, as true as the reality of God's grace and mercy. It's another gift.

You and I do *not* have the capacity—the understanding—to receive God's grace. On our own, we are not wise enough to figure out that we are eternally lost and in desperate need of being found. We need a second gift to complete the transaction.

The Second Gift. Faith to believe is the second gift. When all hell breaks loose, we may know where the hospital (grace) is, but we need the power to get there (faith). When the lights have gone out, we know that we have flashlights and plenty of fresh batteries (grace), but we need the wisdom to locate them (faith to believe).

One of the first Bible verses my mother helped me memorize as a small boy says it clearly. But there was no way I could grasp all of its power back then. "For it is by grace you have been saved, through faith—and *this* not from yourselves, it is the gift of God—not by works, so that no one can boast."[3] *Eph. 2: 8-9*

Once we understand who Jesus is and what He did, it's plain to see that God's grace is nothing we could have done on our own. It's this grace that satisfies a perfect God's anger over sinfulness . . . and rescues us in our lostness. It's a gift.

But believing and receiving is something that we cannot do. We can't believe in or receive God's grace without faith. So faith is the second gift God provides.

Look at the verses again. God freely gives us His grace. Grace rescued us. And we receive His grace through faith, but having faith is God's gift to us as well. We *must* receive them both.

Tucked into the Bible's most poignant chapter about people of faith—sometimes called the Great Hall of Faith—is this verse: "Without faith it is impossible to please God, because anyone who comes to him must believe that he exists and that he rewards those who earnestly seek him."[4]

So here's the puzzle. Faith is a requirement . . . but it's only attainable as a gift from God. *Heb. 11: 6*

Take a moment and read that sentence again. *Faith is a requirement . . . but it's only attainable as a gift from God.*

How can something that's not optional be *impossible* to do? Only when that unattainable thing comes to us as a gift.

Two Men with Their Eyes Wide Open

It was Sunday afternoon. Resurrection day.

Earlier that day, Jesus had suprised Mary Magdalene, Salome, and Mary, James's mother. The women had come to anoint Jesus' dead body with spices, but a radiant angel appeared just outside the tomb, telling them that Jesus was alive. As they ran to tell the disciples the news, Someone else stepped into their path.

"Greetings," the Man said.

It was Jesus.

Alive.

The women were awestruck. They looked into His face and saw that it was really Him.

"Jesus?" they gasped. They were so overcome that they fell to the ground.

"Do not be afraid," Jesus said, trying to calm them. "Go and tell my brothers to go to Galilee; there they will see me."[5]

But when the women told Peter and John the news, the eager men couldn't wait for Galilee. They ran with all their might to the empty tomb to see for themselves.

Word traveled quickly that Jesus was alive. But some missed it.

That very afternoon, two men were walking the seven-mile journey from Jerusalem to Emmaus. Though they had been among Jesus' followers, somehow they had not heard the news of His resurrection. As friends often do, these men were sharing their sorrow with each other. Discussing the tragic events of the past few days, their gloomy faces revealed their sadness.

Suddenly another man caught up with these travelers and joined them on the road. He asked what they had been talking about and why they looked so downcast.

Surprised that anyone in the area could have *not* heard the news of the trial, the beating, and the crucifixion of the man named Jesus, the two friends reviewed what had happened. They recounted every detail with their new walking companion. It was Jesus, but they did not recognize Him.

As you and I read this story, it begs an obvious question. If these men had *really* known Jesus, heard Him speak and seen His miracles, why didn't they recognize Him that afternoon?

The straightforward answer is found at the beginning of the story: "Their eyes *were prevented* from recognizing Him."[6]

Did you catch it? They were *prevented* from seeing who He was. It wasn't that they hadn't been paying attention to what Jesus looked like when they were with Him. Of course they knew what He looked like. It wasn't that they weren't doing their best to figure out who this Stranger was. Naturally, they would have looked Him over as He joined them in their trek to Emmaus.

These two men didn't recognize the Master because something was clouding their eyesight. Maybe like when a person's face is electronically obscured on TV when the producer wants to hide his identity. As Cleopas and his companion looked at Jesus, something scrambled their vision. Outside of their direct control, the two men were kept from recognizing Jesus.

When they finally arrived at their destination, the two men invited the Stranger to join them for dinner and lodging. Jesus agreed.

As they reclined at the table, Jesus picked up some bread, gave thanks, tore off a piece, and handed it to the men. *Luke 24:31*

"Then their eyes *were opened* and they knew Him; and He vanished from their sight."[7] In the same way that the men's eyes—not by their own choice—had been restrained, *now* their eyes were opened—not by their own power. Someone had provided them with the capacity to see.

The ability to recognize Jesus for who He is, to believe that He paid the ultimate price for our sins, and to receive His amazing grace is a free gift. It is not something you and I are capable to see on our own. We cannot earn it. Our intelligence, our experience, even our desire to see doesn't get it done. Only our willingness to receive God's gift of faith opens our eyes and hearts to receive the gift of His grace.

Seek and you shall find

Help Me, Please!

Another story that underscores that faith is a gift is the Bible account of the desperate father of a sick son in the book of Mark, chapter 9. From a young age, the boy was a victim of violent and repeated seizures. Convinced that these uncontrollable convulsions were the result of an evil spirit, the father brought the lad to the Master for healing.

"If You can do anything," the father pleaded with Jesus, "have mercy on us and help us!"

"*If* You can?'" Jesus said, repeating the father's words. "All things are possible to him who believes."

"I do believe," the dad impulsively responded. Then unveiling the doubt lurking in his heart, he added, "Help my unbelief."[8] *Luke 9:22-24*

The pleading father brought the boy to Jesus because he knew Jesus *could* heal his son, but he needed help in believing that Jesus *would* heal him. So the dad asked the Savior to give him the gift of faith.

"I'm not strong enough. By myself, I'm not capable of believing that You will heal my son," he was saying. "I have a little bit of faith. But I need more. Please help me to believe."

A Quick Look Back

In the previous chapters we have looked at four essentials, four things we'd better have nailed down. We talked about the important fact that *God is God*, examining the wonder of creation, His character and activity, and His mercy. We looked at the Bible and identified it as *God's Word*. We discussed our *lostness* and the fact that *Jesus lived, died, and rose again to save lost people like us*.

"But what if I can't believe any of this?" you might ask. "It sounds like pure fiction to me . . . all of it."

You're not alone. That is exactly the starting place for every believer. No one has the ability to believe a single bit of it. Only after we receive the gift called faith are we *able* to believe.

"Dear God," we ask. "I want the gift of faith. If all this is true, then please make it clear to me. I want to believe. Please give me the gift of faith so I *can*."

Then What Happens?

When God grants us the gift of faith—the ability to believe—something happens that is both wonderful and frightening. Like the men lounging at dinner in Emmaus, when our eyes are opened, then we see Jesus for who He is—*and* we see ourselves. We see His goodness, and we also become painfully aware of our own failure and lostness.

So it's a natural consequence: when we receive the gift of faith—when our eyes are opened and we see into our own hearts—repentance is right around the corner.

> *We see His goodness, and we also become painfully aware of our own failure and lostness.*

Among the many biblical examples of remorse and repentance, perhaps the best known is the story of the miscreant who confronted his father, requesting his inheritance. "I wish you were dead," the brash youngster might as well have said. "I want my money right now."

The father relented, giving his son the portion of his estate that would have been his. His bags packed, the boy headed off to a distant country. Like anyone with more cold cash than common sense, there he squandered his money.

Then two very bad things happened: the wild young man reached the bottom of his money pouch, and a famine broke out in the land. Not only did his wealth disappear, but so did the job market, his only hope for financial recovery. The best he could do was land a job out in the field, feeding garbage to pigs. Remember, this boy had a loving, wealthy, and generous father somewhere. But by his *own* decision, he was far from home and slopping hogs. It is one of history's most graphic portraits of lostness.

Then something remarkable happened. The boy's eyes *were opened.* Receiving this gift of faith was surely the answer to his father's earnest prayers. "Sovereign Lord," the dad must have pleaded, "please help my son to see. Please give him faith to believe that I love him and want him to come home."

And then the father's longing was miraculously satisfied. The Bible account says, "When [the young man] came to his senses, he said, 'How many of my father's hired men have food to spare, and here I am starving to death! I will set out and go back to my father and say to him: Father, I have sinned against heaven and against you. I am no longer worthy to be called your son; make me like one of your hired men.' So he got up and went to his father."[9] Luke 15:17-20

Here's what actually happened to this runaway: *the prodigal looked at himself the way God (and everyone else) saw him.*

One of the sobering realities of marriage and parenthood is the way they shine a revealing light on who we really are. When our daughters were small and I corrected them without much tenderness, Bobbie would take me aside. Her mission was to tell me what she had just seen. She may not have had a problem with *what* I had done in disciplining our children but *how* I had done it.

"You were right to challenge the girls on their behavior," she would say to me, "but you should have seen your unforgiving face and heard your condescending tone of voice."

Defensive, I sometimes accused my wife of spoiling for a fight. Unwilling to admit the truth about myself that was driving my children away from me. Self-righteousness—my stubborn refusal to open my eyes and see myself in the mirror—was the cause.

Private, after-dinner conversations with Bobbie would go like this:

Bobbie: When you corrected the girls about their table manners, you had a scowl on your face that looked cruel.

Me: What do mean, "scowl"?

Bobbie: You know what I'm talking about. Reprimanding the girls about the way they were acting at the table, that was okay. But the sneer on top of it was unnecessary.

Me: Now you've moved from *scowl* to *sneer*. Which is it?

Bobbie: Why do you do that?

Me: Do what?

If you've been in a similar situation, you know how difficult and painful it is to own up to the truth. To see ourselves as others see us.

Anyone watching the prodigal son during his wild odyssey would have his seen his carefree "high life" turn into a pile of rubbish.

Then, one day, through newly opened eyes, the young man saw his situation for what it was. He spoke the truth. "All of my father's servants have plenty of food," he said to himself. "But I am here, almost dying with hunger."[10] Luke 15:17

There's nothing profound about these words. They're a simple, straightforward fact. Until that moment, he didn't see himself as God—and others—saw him. His eyes needed to be opened.

The prodigal agreed with God that he was in trouble.

It's interesting how the expression "consenting adults" seems to be all that's necessary to turn perilously destructive behavior into something acceptable. "As long as no one gets hurt" falls into the same category.

The son feeding the swine did not choose an "I'm a victim and can't help myself" mentality. He would have none of that. The speech he rehearsed for his father is honest and precise: "I have sinned against heaven and you."

When our eyes are opened and we see ourselves from God's perspective, we admit that even if there is another consenting adult involved, our sin is against a holy God in heaven.

A thousand years before the prodigal's story was told, King David summarized his sins of adultery and murder with these words: "I know my transgressions, and my sin is ever before me. Against You, You only, I have sinned and done what is evil in Your sight."[11]

Like the young man who ran away from home with his inheritance stashed in his back pocket, David also saw his own recklessness and came to his senses. His eyes were opened and he was able to take a step back and see his own situation: "I know my transgressions, and my sin is ever before me." David saw himself through God's eyes. "Against *You* I have sinned."

It doesn't matter what consenting adults may say. With the gift of faith, you and I see the *complete* picture. When we see ourselves from God's view, his opinion becomes the standard that matters.

The prodigal made a decision.

Rev. Colin Smith says it this way: "Repentance always begins with a decision."[12]

This isn't about emotionalism. Certainly, emotions play a part when the truth comes out. But this choice comes from a person's will. When we come to terms with our lostness, we decide at a specific moment in time to do something about it. We make a *decision* to turn around and go in a different direction. This is called *repentance*.

Not long ago, I met a young husband and father who had come to his senses. Over the previous twelve months, he had been frequenting pornographic websites. Once occasional and casual visits had become an uncontrollable obsession. One day, facing his wife's sincere questioning, the man realized what he was doing.

This is killing me, he concluded, taking an honest inventory of himself. *And it's killing my family.*

So he made a decision to stop. Repentance always begins with a decision.

Like the prodigal, his eyes were opened. He saw himself and his activity as God saw it. He was disgusted by his own sin. He repented of his vile obsession—to God and to his wife. He also called others in his immediate circle of friends and family to confess his sin to them. As if seeing himself in the mirror, he finally came to his senses, and doing something about it was a painful experience. But because of the awfulness he saw in his behavior, he was determined to change.

He asked a handful of close friends to help hold him to his resolution. He even changed his Internet password to "J-E-S-U-S." There would be no escaping who it was that brought him to his senses and who would empowered him to change.

When all hell broke loose in his life, the family man made a decision.

Today this young man counsels others in his town who need their eyes to be opened to truth. He prays with them and for them to have their eyes opened by a loving heavenly Father.

The prodigal humbled himself.

The prodigal's speech to his father includes a statement of contrition and humility: "I am no longer worthy to be called your son."

Some may accuse the young man of sales-speak, of memorizing a little script to get him what he wanted. Like Eddie Haskell in the classic television episodes of *Leave It to Beaver*, the prodigal was just polishing the apple for Ward and June Cleaver. Perhaps.

But remember that the wayward son was preparing to speak to his father, the same dad to whom he had essentially said, "I wish you were dead." This was a situation where both the father and son knew exactly what had happened. "I am no longer worthy to be called your son" sure sounds like an expression of genuine humility and contrition.

The prodigal spoke his confession.

What can ever compete with the incredible power of words? Using the effect of what rolls off our tongues as a metaphor, the apostle James said, "If we put the bits into the horses' mouths so that they will obey us, we direct their entire body as well. Look at the ships also, though they are so great and are driven by strong winds, are still directed by a very small rudder wherever the inclination of the pilot desires. So also the tongue is a small part of the body, and yet it boasts of great things."[13] *James 3:3-5*

You and I could ruin a lifetime of building an admirable reputation in a matter of seconds. With a few words, we could forever cripple a priceless relationship or destroy our careers. It doesn't seem fair, does it? But we know it's true.

Regret can be expressed with a shrug, rolled eyes, and a facial expression of chagrin. Remorse can be expressed with a grunt of "Uh, hey . . . sorry." But true repentance articulated in specific words and measured tones is much more believable—and forgivable.

The apostle Paul talks about the importance of *saying* words of repentance. "If you confess *with your mouth* the Lord Jesus and believe in your heart that God has raised Him from the dead, you will be saved. For . . . *with the mouth* confession is made unto salvation."[14] The prodigal didn't return to his father with a shrug or a grunt. He admitted the truth in specific words to his father. *Rom. 10:9-10*

Read ## Where Does This Bring Us?

In this chapter we've talked about God's double gift. His gift of grace and His gift of faith that enables us to believe. We have underscored that this kind of faith gives us a new set of eyes to see God, and also to see ourselves as we really are. The improved vantage point of clear vision leads us to repentance, which always begins with a decision. And we've looked at some examples of what the decision to repent looks like.

You might ask at this point, "What difference will these words of repentance make? How will God react to my confession? What will He say when I speak the words? What will happen to my heart?"

Dr. Ravi Zacharias tells a story about the sweetness of repentance. When he was a young boy, living in his homeland of India, he loved two things: playing cricket with his friends and eating, especially sweets. Any available time was spent playing, and any available cash was spent on food, especially sweets! Boys.

Ravi tells the story of buying ice cream from a street vendor's cart. The cart, fixed to the front of a bicycle, was manned by a quite rotund and happy Sikh.

Young Ravi selected the ice cream he wanted and gave the man a note worth five rupees. Receiving his change, Ravi looked into his hand and realized that the vendor had made a mistake. The money was change from ten rupees instead of five.

I have just made five rupees, Ravi thought to himself, and he hurried off to enjoy his treat.

But the ice cream was not as sweet as he had hoped. His good fortune tasted more like bitter thievery than luck.

"Each time I saw the ice cream man in the weeks that followed," Ravi writes in his memoirs, "I struggled inside." *I stole from that man,* he said to himself.[15]

Try as he might to get over the incident, Ravi could not escape the wrongness of what he had done. So, with boyish determination, he made a decision.

"I saved up every coin I could, from here and there, for several months," Ravi writes. "And I went back to the man. Very respectfully I said, 'Sir, I have to ask you to forgive me for something. I made a big mistake. You gave me more change for an ice cream some time ago than you should have.'"

A waiting silence ensued. Would the man clobber or berate him? The stillness pried open more of the boy's shame.

"I would be willing to give you more than what you gave me back because," Ravi stammered, "I've had your money all this while."

Ravi writes, "When I raised my eyes, I saw that he didn't know what to do. He was profoundly moved and almost in a state of shock. He took the money I held out to him. He may have offered me a free ice cream in return; I don't remember. All I know is, as I turned to go home, a huge burden had rolled off my shoulders."[16]

We know this feeling, don't we? Its sweetness is indescribable—knowing that we've done the right thing in spite of our desire to hide the truth and keep the "stolen" money for ourselves.

But what does a holy God do with our repentance? Does He stand in silence, as the icecream vendor did? Does He react at all? Isn't it His right to crush us? Or, at least, shame us?

Fortunately, we don't have to wonder. In telling the story of the runaway boy, Jesus shines the light on God's attitude toward us. As a picture of God's response to our repentance, Jesus tells us about the prodigal's father.

God Rushes to Welcome Us When We Return.

There are many colorful images in the Bible: the creation of the world, spun from nothing by the sound of God's voice; Noah and his family saved from the ravages of the Flood in a homemade boat, packed wall to wall with reeking animals; two sides of the Red Sea, standing at attention so the Israelites can pass between them and escape the pursuing Egyptian army; the impenetrable walls of Jericho crumbling into a pile of rubble; and Elijah's altar consumed by fire from heaven.

But the heart-rending drama of the father running down the lane to greet his returning son has no rival.

Someone has said that there are very few times in Scripture where God is in a hurry. But here's an example. God is in a hurry to *forgive*. He is eager to welcome a repentant child home.

God's embrace . . . feeling forgiven as well as knowing it

A careful look at the way this scene of reconciliation is pretty revealing. "But while he was still a long way off, his father saw him and felt compassion for him, and ran and embraced him and kissed him."[17]

> But the heart-rending drama of the father running down the lane to greet his returning son has no rival.

Who did the embracing? Who did the kissing? Look again; who took the initiative?

Can you picture the contrite lad, his clothes looking like rags and his arms still hanging at his side, being lavished with affection from a father who must have wondered if his son would ever return? Can you imagine the boy's thoughts as this was going on? Dreading the possibility of his father's unsympathetic response, he had braced himself for the punishment he deserved. Instead, the son stands there on the road, smothered in his dad's forgiveness.

The condition of our heart is more important than the eloquence of our tongue

I love to picture the prodigal on his journey home. Rehearsing his speech as he walks, he repeats the phrases over and over, hoping to communicate his sincere repentance with passion.

"Father . . . I am *no* longer worthy to be called your son; make me as one of your hired men . . ."

"Father . . . I am no *longer* worthy to be called your son; make me as one of your hired men . . ."

"Father . . . I am no longer *worthy* to be called your son; make me as one of your hired men . . ."

But once the father had finished his embrace, he didn't even give the boy enough time to finish the well-rehearsed contrition speech. That really cinching, penitent part about being willing to become the father's servant never hit the air.

Just by the son's willingness to return home, the father knew the decision the boy had made. Repentance was evident and far more important than the eloquence—or even the completion—of the speech.

The prodigal may have started his memorized chatter, but it was drowned out by his father ordering the servants to prepare a homecoming feast. Just envision how grateful—and overwhelmed—the son was to realize the reliability and security of his father's love.

God's grace is a lavish gift.

"Give the lad a corned beef sandwich on rye, with a pickle and a side of chips" would have been more than the prodigal deserved. It surely would have been more than he expected.

But the father ordered all work to stop and an extravagant dinner to be prepared in the boy's honor.

It was not a reluctant "All right, I'll give you one more chance . . . *just* one more." The father issued instructions to make ready a *celebration*.

"Quickly, bring the best robe . . . put a ring on his finger and brand-new sandals on his feet. Kill the fattened calf, the one we've been saving for a time like this. My son was dead but has come to life again; he was lost but now has been found."[18]

Can you crawl into the boy's skin and experience what all this commotion must have felt like? Any awkwardness and embarrassment is replaced by stunning awareness of the celebration for him. The boy's faith placed in the father's grace made him the guest of honor—the reason for the party.

Isn't It Time?

The story's ending is not a surprise. You may have heard it many times. So you know that genuine confession and repentance leads to celebration.

Why don't you pick up the phone right now and call that person you need to forgive, someone with whom you have a broken relationship that needs mending? It's easier for someone to forgive when approached by someone with a contrite heart. Although our words may falter, we know that the decision we make and the condition of our hearts will be more persuasive than our words.

It's time to kneel before our heavenly Father and confess our sin—anything that draws us away or displeases Him. Though we're aware of what we've done, He is the only One who knows what's *really* going on inside: the bitterness, the rage, the hatred, the pride, the desire to succeed at others' expense, the greed, the lack of compassion. He knows our hearts and is ready to forgive so we can be free to celebrate.

So why don't we?

Because we can't. We cannot take these steps of repentance and confession and contrition on our own . . . not without receiving the gift of faith.

Several years ago, at a family reunion, my brother, Dan, led the morning devotions. He drew from a story in Luke 8, the one about Jesus calming the storm. The account begins with something I hadn't seen before.

"One day Jesus said to his disciples, 'Let's go over to the other side of the lake.'"[19]

Getting into the boat was clearly Jesus' idea. And because He is God, Jesus knew that they were headed into a squall. The storm was not a surprise

Luke 8:22-25

to Him. He also knew that the disciples were going to be terrified. Putting them in the middle of a dangerous situation was *Jesus'* idea.

Immediately after He stood up on the boat's stern and rebuked the storm, Jesus turned to His disciples and said, "Where is your faith?"[20] On their own, they didn't have any faith, and at that moment—as hellish waves were breaking loose—they knew it full well. That was the idea.

Let the Games Begin

As you know, the goal of this book is to help take you to the place of crisis *before* you get there, *before* all hell breaks loose, so you can prepare. It's about packing your lunch before you're hungry, stocking up on fresh batteries before the lights go out, backing up your computer before the hard drive crashes.

In the spring of 2005, I was doing what I've done countless times: hurrying from one gate to the next at the massive and sprawling DFW airport to change planes. Of course, DFW is so big that it has its own zip code.

As my cell phone rang from inside my briefcase, I stopped long enough to unzip it from its home, strapped neatly to my wheeled suitcase.

The number on the caller ID was a familiar one.

"Hi, honey," I said to my wife, continuing on my journey to C33. "How are you?"

"Fine," she replied, but I could tell she didn't call for small talk. Don't ask me how I knew after just one word, but I did.

"Robert," she said, her voice dropping, "I just heard from your doctor." She took a short breath. "You have skin cancer."

I stopped midstride. Folks who had been keeping pace behind me swerved to avoid a pileup right there in the middle of the concourse. I paid no attention to their momentary inconvenience.

Cold chills ran down my body. As if the world had ground to slow motion, I heard the words again, without Bobbie even speaking: "You . . . have . . . cancer."

I didn't say anything, but Bobbie could hear the typical chatter of the airport's loudspeaker over my cell phone, so she knew we were still connected.

"The biopsy came back positive," she said. "I have you scheduled for surgery as soon as they can fit you in."

Because we live in Orange County, Florida, the skin-cancer capital of America, visits to the dermatologist are scheduled like dental checkups. Regularly. I had noticed a little spot above my right eyebrow. It first showed up after I had trimmed some bushes in my backyard. I thought a branch had scraped my forehead.

But a week later it looked the same. Another week passed. No change.

So we scheduled an appointment. The doctor's associate numbed the area and sliced off a tiny piece of skin to send to the lab.

What amazed me was that immediately after the biopsy, my forehead healed. The spot almost disappeared. I was relieved and confident that there was nothing to worry about.

"No problem, Mr. Wolgemuth," I envisioned them saying. "Just a routine exam. It's good that you took the time to get it checked out."

I continued to walk toward my gate, but my stride was slow and measured.

"Don't you mean 'precancerous'?" I questioned Bobbie, drawing from something I had heard the nurse say.

"No," Bobbie said, never one to cower to diplomacy at critical moments like this. "It's cancer."

"Let me call you back when I get to C33," I said.

My suitcase followed me along the tiled floor toward my gate, the *clickety-clack* of the wheels providing an eerie and solemn rhythm.

But between Bobbie's phone call and my arrival at C33, I felt as though I was walking onto the field of play. I was no longer a spectator, sitting in the stands. The ball was in my hands, and I was in the game.

I thought of my wife and my children and my grandchildren. Then my mind was drawn to my dad, who had died a few years earlier. I thought about my mother dealing with her loss. I reviewed the condition of my will and important papers, suddenly wanting to make certain that Bobbie knew where everything was filed.

And I thought about God. Everything I believed was on the line. It was game time.

A Little Revival at C33

Arrival at the departure gate left me with plenty of time before my next flight. This time a short delay was welcome. I had promised to call Bobbie, but before I did, I found a seat facing the windows and the tarmac. Huge jets lumbered back and forth. Like busy caterpillars, baggage wagons hurried about.

I leaned back in the chair and crossed my arms. *I'm sorry,* I said to God in silent prayer. *I have been in such a hurry that I've set You aside. Forgive me for the sin of squeezing You out of my frenzied life.*

I sat in silence for a while, rehearsing the past fifteen minutes and how calm I actually felt in that moment.

What was I thinking? That thought made me smile. *Thank You for getting my attention,* I added. *This is a gift from You.* I took in a deep breath and let it out. *Please forgive me.*

I called Bobbie, a more peaceful person than the one who had spoken to her a few minutes earlier. A lump formed in my throat when I heard her voice. I told her that I was at peace about everything and that her news had given me a renewed look at God's providence and good gifts.

As it turned out, the crisis was minor. The visit to the doctor and subsequent surgical extraction of the cancer cells were hardly momentous. The surgeon assured me that he had "gotten it all."

But like the boy standing on the farm lane, in tattered clothes and his arms at his side, I had experienced the warmth of forgiveness—the embrace—of My Father. The forgiveness was real. The closeness I felt to Him was where I longed to stay.

> *Through our confusion and fear, we receive His peace and the gift of faith.*

"Come to Me," Jesus said, "all [you] who are weary and heavy-laden, and I will give you rest."[21]

You are I are never drawn closer to God than when we're without resources—in the place of humility and repentance. And getting us to that place is God's special gift.

When the busyness of our lives comes to a screaming and unpredicted halt, when we enter His presence and in the stillness ask for it . . . that's when we receive the gift. Through our confusion and fear, we receive His peace and the gift of faith.

Back to Caesarea Philippi

In the last chapter we looked at the intimate conversation Jesus had with His disciples. When Peter had boldly blurted out that He was the Messiah.

Jesus had said to Peter, "You are blessed, Simon son of Jonah, because no person taught you that. My Father in heaven showed you who I am."[22]

Jesus could have complimented Peter on his perception and his courage to speak up. But the truth is, Peter didn't have the skill or insight to declare Jesus as the Messiah, even after years of spending time with the Savior and witnessing countless miracles. Instead, Jesus was saying to the bold fisherman, "Well done, my friend. You have received the gift of faith." In other words, "You didn't come up with this truth on your own. It came to you as a gift. Congratulations on receiving it."

Grace, through His Son, is one of God's amazing gifts to you and me. And faith—the ability to see ourselves through new eyes, to repent, to

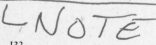

NOTE

draw close to Him, to feel His embrace and to receive this gift of grace—
is another gift.

These two gifts are ours for the receiving. Jesus said when describing the
persistence of a person who truly wants the good things the Father has for
us, "Ask, and it will be given to you; seek, and you will find; knock, and it
will be opened to you. For everyone who asks receives, and he who seeks
finds, and to him who knocks it will be opened."[23]   *Luke 11:9-10*

Setting the Nail

The first few things that you and I must nail down challenged our thinking, our presuppositions. "God is God" gave us a bigger picture of a holy,
sovereign, and merciful Creator and a more realistic perspective of who we
are as His children. The marvelous miracle of the Bible—its origin, how it
has been preserved, and its cultural impact for centuries—was explained.

Then we talked about the irrefutable truth of our lostness and God's
provision in sending Jesus to pay the price for our sin, a price that the funds
in our bank accounts will never be sufficient to cover. Again, these are
issues that can be discussed with some sense of reason and objectivity.

But this fifth thing, that grace and faith are gifts, doesn't give us as
much space for intellectualizing. As the old preacher admitted to his congregation at the close of a particularly intense sermon, "We've gone from
preachin' to meddlin'."

When we're in the vortex of the storm, of course it's important to have
the foundation of our thinking on solid footing . . . God, the Bible, and
Jesus. But what about our heart condition when all hell breaks loose? Where
is our hope? Or as Jesus asked His hysterical disciples when the swells and
waves were crashing over the gunnels of the boat, where is our faith?

The simple answer is this: we don't have any. Emotions build up inside
that could grip us with overwhelming fear and despair. As if we've been

attacked by a flu virus, our stomachs tighten in pain, our bodies ache, and our heads swim with dizziness. Sometimes we're too scared to cry out, too stunned to weep.

"This isn't happening to me," we whisper.

But it is. All hell has broken loose.

So, like the panicked disciples, you and I crawl to the feet of Jesus and confess, "I wasn't ready for this. I'm blinded with fear. God, I *know* You can comfort and heal. I know You've done this for others, and I know You are in control."

You take a deep breath. "Now, please, Father, give me faith to believe."

And He will.

THE SIXTH THING
TO HAVE NAILED DOWN:

Belief and Works Are One

Before Bobbie and I moved to our neighborhood in February 2000, we knew none of the people on our street. Though today we can call most of the folks by name, none of our neighbors attended our wedding in 1970, thirty years before we moved here. We didn't invite a single one. Of course, none of them actually had to be at our wedding to know that we're married. We've given them good reasons to assume it.

We both wear wedding bands. We walk our dog around the neighborhood every day, holding hands, unless it's too hot to hold hands. (Have you ever been to Florida in the summer?) Because we've hosted many neighborhood meetings and celebrations, some neighbors have visited Bobbie and me inside our home. They've seen pictures of our family, and have met our children and grandchildren when our kids have visited us from North Carolina.

These people, complete strangers before we relocated here, have no doubt that one day, my wife and I got married.

What happened in 1970 is a fact. Bobbie and I stood in the chancel at

Cherrydale Baptist Church in Arlington, Virginia, and made our vows. We exchanged rings, and Pastor A. W. Jackson pronounced us "husband and wife."

I planted the traditional kiss, and we were off. And because the words we had spoken meant something, we moved in together, shared meals together, and even slept together. Our vows sealed our marriage, and we did something about it.

We could say that our words and our lifestyle match; the two are connected.

We aren't married on Mondays, Wednesdays, and Fridays *only*. We don't take vacations from our marriage—only from holding hands on our summer walks. And though we have our disagreements, we don't announce that "right now, marriage isn't very fun, so we're going to take a day off."

It's the very same in our walk with Christ. What we believe and how we act should be in agreement. Our beliefs and our actions—often called "works" in the Bible—are one.

This may not sound like a huge, spellbinding, crank-turning notion— that beliefs and works are inseparable—but it's a very important truth to consider as we take time to nail down the essentials.

Don't Tell Martin Luther It's Not Important

On October 31, 1517, a young monk posted a document on the door of the Castle Church at Wittenberg, Germany. Angered by the activity of some of the leaders in the Roman Catholic Church, Luther wrote his infamous 95 Theses, starting a brush fire that turned into a raging blaze. It changed the world.

The first of these ninety-five declarations was "When our Lord and Master, Jesus Christ, said 'Repent,' He called for the entire life of believers to be one of repentance."

What was Luther dealing with in the early sixteenth century? With the words "the entire life of believers," Luther was condemning the church's practice of "indulgences."

Indulgences may have actually started out to be an honorable thing—a statement by the Roman church that "belief and works are one." When a person received God's grace through faith, his good deeds of service—his indulgences—were the visible sign of his interior commitment.

Here's where the church got creative: Doing something "good" was pronounced a necessary punishment for sins committed. But average church-goers with busy lives didn't really have time to visit widows and orphans, give to the poor, or assist the weak. So the church began to market indulgences—to put good works up for sale. And much like giving a few dollars to a high school boy to mow your lawn instead of mowing it yourself, indulgences were a way to pay instead of play. "Get out of jail free" cards were for sale.

Since priests were full-time good-deed doers, they had warehouses full of indulgence inventories. Ordinary people were absolved in exchange for money instead of repenting of their sins and cleaning up their lives.

The sale of indulgences was happening right under Luther's nose. Some of his own parishioners in Germany stopped attending church because a fellow priest, Johann Tetzel, was selling them get-out-of-church-free indulgences. Martin Luther was infuriated.

It's no wonder these indulgences were so popular. A common parishioner caught doing wrong or neglecting church could avoid punishment. Anyone accused of hitting his kids or living in sin could level the score with God by buying an indulgence. It was as easily as snatching up a bargain at the corner apothecary. The buyer could be counted as a righteous person after making the investment. The church trafficked in satisfying guilty consciences with cash. Really wealthy folks provided the mother lode.

"You don't have to actually live your beliefs," the church was saying.

"Good works can be subcontracted to the professionals for a small fee." Sometimes a not-so-small fee was solicited to balance out a really big sin . . . again, rich guys equaled advantage.

It was this blatant inconsistency between belief and truly good works that triggered Luther's outrage. "You can't join the pay-as-you-sin plan," he was saying. "If you're truly repentant, then your *entire life* must be consistent with your beliefs."

Not a Problem Anymore?

It's probably been awhile since you've heard of someone actually claiming to have his or her sins forgiven by writing a check, but the danger—and temptation—of separating faith and works into two categories is as up to date as this morning's weather report.

Treating our beliefs and our conduct as two different commodities is as dangerous as ignoring a shooting chest pain or not fastening our seat belts in high-speed traffic.

As followers of Jesus Christ, how we live—the words we say, our relationships with others, what goes on in our minds, how we act in public, how we treat our families, *and* what we're like when no one else is around—must be in harmony with what we say we believe.

The apostle James left no doubt about his belief in this truth.

What good is it, my brothers, if a man claims to have faith but has no deeds? Can such faith save him? Suppose a brother or sister is without clothes and daily food. If one of you says to him, "Go, I wish you well; keep warm and well fed," but does nothing about his physical needs, what good is it? In the same way, faith by itself, if it is not accompanied by action, is dead. . . . As the body without the spirit is dead, so faith without deeds is dead.[1] James 2:14–17; 26

What we believe must be verified, confirmed, and demonstrated by what we do.

"If you get married," James could have said, "live like a married person. Talk, think, and act married. You're not single anymore. After the wedding, go ahead and move in together. Show people that your life is going to be different by sharing an address."

Being married but living separately would be inconsistent.

The apostle Paul agrees with this view of matching beliefs with actions: "Whether you eat or drink, or whatever you do, do all to the glory of God."[2]

1 Cor. 10:31

What Qualifies as "All"?

What qualifies as "all," as in, "do *all*" to God's glory?

Let's look at the answer this way. There are 24 hours in your day and seven days in your week. That means you have exactly 168 hours in your week. The circle below represents those 168 hours.

Now let's divide the circle into sections that represent the way we spend those hours. If we get our full recommended daily allowance of sleep—8 hours a day—that's 56 hours, or one-third of the available hours. If we have full-time, salaried jobs, there's at least another 40 hours. We're up to 96 of the 168 hours (more if you're a homemaker).

The rest of our available hours are spent in various ways: 10.5 hours for morning and evening grooming (a total of one and a half hours a day); 17.5 hours eating (a half hour for breakfast and an hour each for lunch and dinner); 8 hours for faith-related activities—Bible reading, prayer, church attendance, etc.; and so on. Thirty-six hours that are left in our week are taken up in commuting, reading, shopping, spending time with our spouses, conversation with friends, civic assignments, sports, and other play.

Given this information, our week looks something like this:

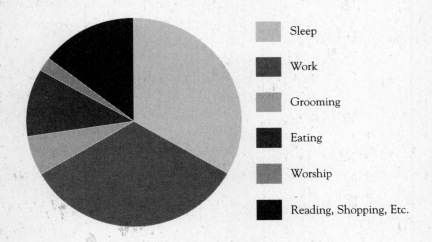

Sleep

Work

Grooming

Eating

Worship

Reading, Shopping, Etc.

Now, according to 1 Corinthians 10:31, which of the above hours can be counted as "all," as in, "do *all* to the glory of God"?

Right. *All* of them.

The eight hours we've set aside for "spiritual activity" are only a start. There should be *no* hours in our week when our activity should not be done to God's glory. *None.*

When we're in a business meeting, when we're hanging out with our closest friends, when we're surfing the Internet, when we're doing our taxes, when it's dark outside, when we're in traffic, when we're sitting in church . . . "all" is *all*.

Because Christ has found us and we have heard the call to follow Him, there should be nothing in our week that isn't covered by what we believe.

There should be no *hours in our week when our activity should not be done to God's glory.* None.

So, what evidence in the everyday moments of our lives mark us as Christ-followers?

For years, Christian books have been challenging us to take our faith to the marketplace, to be "salt" and "light" as Jesus commanded in the Sermon on the Mount.[3] They dare us to live and act and work in such a way that God is honored and people are drawn to Him by our example.

Being a Christ-follower at work may mean placing a Bible on the corner of your desk or saying a blessing before you eat lunch with your colleagues. But it's much more than that. Read what Paul said about our behavior as Christians. Then look at it in light of your workplace.

Don't just pretend that you love others. Really love them. Hate what is wrong. Stand on the side of the good. Love each other with genuine affection, and take delight in honoring each other. Never be lazy in your work, but serve the Lord enthusiastically.

Be glad for all God is planning for you. Be patient in trouble, and always be prayerful. When God's children are in need, be the one to help them out. And get into the habit of inviting guests home for dinner or, if they need lodging, for the night.

If people persecute you because you are a Christian, don't curse them; pray that God will bless them. When others are happy, be happy with them. If they are sad, share their sorrow. Live in harmony with each other. Don't try to act important, but enjoy the company of ordinary people. And don't think you know it all![4]

It might be helpful to take a piece of paper and write down some of the specific ways that you could put some of the above challenges to work, *at work*. What would these admonitions look like if they were applied to the place where you spend most of your waking hours during the week?

Stand on the side of good; take delight in honoring each other; never be lazy; be patient in trouble; live in harmony; and don't try to act important. *Hmm . . .*

Paul's instructions provide a brilliant checklist for us to follow at work. The evidence of our walk with Christ should be visible in everything we do.

"All" is *all*.

The Not-So-Balanced Life

From 1969 through 1976, Bobbie and I were involved in a youth ministry called Youth for Christ as a career. We loved the teenagers and enjoyed sharing our faith with them during those years.

Some of the YFC staff leaders began to promote a concept called "the balanced life." They took their cue from Luke 2:52 (NIV): "And Jesus grew in wisdom and stature, and in favor with God and men."

From this verse, which addressed all things mental (wisdom), physical (stature), spiritual (favor with God), and social (favor with man), these leaders created the following diagram:

Mental	Physical
Spiritual	Social

Though the philosophy of this diagram is sound, it could be misleading to an average teenager or even the adult teaching it. They *could* think that the only part of life that needs to be lived to the glory of God is the "spiritual" part. There is danger in thinking that when it comes to the other areas of our lives, we can pretty much do as we please. One-fourth belongs to God; the rest is ours. (In our pie chart above, spiritual activity was only 4.7 percent of our week.)

That simply is not true. Our beliefs and our activities—no matter what they are—*cannot* be lived in isolation from each other.

And It Works Both Ways

The unity between belief and works also means that good deeds are no substitute for faith. Regardless of how exemplary our behavior may be, you and I cannot stack up enough commendable works to turn us into authentic Christ-followers. We cannot buy enough indulgences.

The grace God offers to us through His Son is a gift that can only be received when we come to Him in simple faith. We could fund our church's entire building campaign and then spend the rest of our lives serving the poor . . . and it still wouldn't be enough to make us right with God.

"When the kindness and love of God our Savior appeared," Paul wrote, "he saved us, not because of righteous things we had done, but because of his mercy."[5] This statement follows right on the heels of another verse that shows how we are empowered to live like true followers of Christ, integrating faith and works. "For the grace of God that brings salvation has appeared to all men. It teaches us to say 'No' to ungodliness and worldly passions, and to live self-controlled, upright and godly lives in this present age."[6]

Did you catch that? We can't work our way to saving faith, but if we *have* saving faith, it *must* be evident in how we live and act—or it's not saving faith.

Dealing with the forbidden separation of belief and works has been a lifelong and challenging adventure for me. It goes back to my first church experiences as a little boy.

The Tale of Two Churches

My earliest memories of church are easy to recall because my own dad was the preacher at Fairview Avenue Brethren in Christ Church. Not only that, but three of my uncles were also pastors in the same denomination. Ditto for both of my grandfathers. Pulpits hung from the limbs of our family tree.

Similar to the Mennonites in theology, the Brethren in Christ were strong believers in community and separation from the world.[7] Most of its people did not vote, play cards, or serve in the military. Even the proper dress code was clearly identifiable. Bright colors were frowned upon, and jewelry was strongly condemned. Black and gray and plain were the only acceptable vogue.

One of the more common texts that preachers chose for their messages was the apostle Paul's admonition to the church in Corinth: "Come out from among them, and be ye separate, saith the Lord, and touch not the unclean thing; and I will receive you."[8]

The interesting thing about sermons addressing outward choices was that, as kids, we could survey the audience—not, of course, so blatantly that our parents would catch us gawking—and spot the "sinners." For instance, any woman without something on her head was suspect. (Members would not have considered sitting in worship without wearing simple white coverings.)

We were not the Amish, so our homes had electricity and running water. And driving cars was acceptable, especially black ones.[9] But going to movies, dancing, and drinking were vociferously preached against from the pulpits.

You can imagine the bent of my young concept of Christians. Much of who we were as believers was identified by our contrast with "worldly" people.

When a couple showed up at one of our services, the husband in a flashy sport coat and his wife wearing makeup, a bright dress, and jewelry, they may as well have been wearing placards that read Visitor. Or maybe Lost.

"We're not like them," my grandmother would whisper to my siblings and me after a diplomatic greeting with these visitors following the service.

Christianity is about appearance, I determined as a youngster. *That's* what's important.

Soon, however, my lens was changed and my perspective began to widen.

Our family moved to the Chicago area in the early '50s. My dad was no longer a parish minister; his career took him into full-time parachurch work.

We were unable to find a Brethren in Christ church in our area, so my parents chose a congregation that held to many of our former church's fundamental doctrinal beliefs.

Our route to the Wheaton Evangelical Free Church on Sunday mornings took us past a Christian Reformed Church on Harrison Street, only a couple blocks from our home. Peering out the backseat window, I saw brightly dressed people—including women wearing makeup and jewelry—standing on the church steps. Some of these people were smoking cigarettes as they chatted before going inside.

Although the expression "freaked out" had yet to be introduced to America's lexicon, it would have been a perfect description of my dad's response to these folks. Of course, he was far too discreet to openly express his disdain, so he would make a *tsk-tsk* sound, which my siblings and I clearly understood without interpretation.

It was clear to me that, though these people went to church, they were certainly *not* Christians. This kind of paradox was far too difficult for a young boy to safely settle in his mind.

But the years that followed included my introduction to school friends from "liberal" churches. Sometimes I'd visit their churches, where "freedom in Christ"—my dad referred to it as "license"—was emphasized. The "condition of the heart," they said, was more important than the color of the sport coat. And you love God and obey Him because you *want to*, not because you *must.* This was paradigm-changing stuff.

Spotting real Christians became a far more difficult sport than it had been for me as a little boy. I discovered that a man could *look* righteous and talk like a Christian but be a liar, a cheat, or a philanderer. And I learned that a woman with impeccably coiffed hair and dangling earrings, who looked as though she had stepped off the pages of *Glamour* magazine, could be a saint, leading home Bible studies and introducing her coworkers to Jesus.

As challenging as this was at first, my discovery that belief and works are one has led me to believe that the Brethren in Christ and the Christian Reformed were both wrong . . . and right.

You and I cannot work—driving black cars or white, wearing drab clothes or chic ones, playing cards or refusing, serving in the army or not, drinking or abstaining, smoking or refraining—our way to saving faith. But if we *have* saving faith, as Luther declared, "justification by faith and faith alone," it must be apparent in how we live and act, or it's not saving faith at all.

A Confrontation for the Record Books

It's fascinating how so many of Jesus' confrontations had to do with this issue of beliefs and works—matching what you say with how you act.

Shades of inquiring reporters at press conferences that we see daily on television, an "expert in religious law" addressed Jesus in front of a crowd to "test" Him with a question.

"Teacher, what must I do to receive eternal life?"[10]

What's intriguing to me is that in telling the story, Luke spotted the fact

that the man—some Bible translations call him a lawyer—was not interested in the answer to the question. Far from being a teachable inquirer, he
seemed to be playing a little game of stump-the-prophet.

What's also interesting—and sobering—about this moment is that the
instant the man stood to speak, Jesus knew exactly what he was going to
ask and why. He knew the man was a scholar of the law and unwilling to
be a practitioner.

Leading the man to address the real issue, Jesus asked an easy question
in return, one He knew the man could answer. It would expose his own
hypocrisy.

"What does the law of Moses say?" Jesus asked. "How do you read it?"

Just as you and I would have done when a teacher asked a question we
were prepared for, this lawyer probably took a deep breath and stood a bit
taller. This was going to be his chance to shine.

"You must love the Lord your God with all your heart, all your soul, all
your strength, and all your mind," he responded.

Here was a thorough description of what it takes to gain eternal life.
Like a tennis player driving a ball down the line past his opponent, the
man must have celebrated—if only inside, so as not to violate decorum—
thinking how succinctly he had answered.

So far, so good.

He should have stopped right then, while he was ahead. Instead, he
piously continued.

" . . . and, 'Love your neighbor as yourself.' "

"Right!" Jesus responded. "Do this and you will live!"

But the scholar wasn't finished. Again he insisted on waxing eloquent,
unaware that he was setting a trap for himself. Perhaps he had a reputation
as a clever scholar with a gift for brilliant oration but an unwillingness to
live in a way that paralleled his words. Whatever the case, Luke reveals
something about this law expert's misguided motives.

"The man wanted to justify his actions," he wrote, "so he asked Jesus, 'And who is my neighbor?'"

Did you see it? He wanted to *justify his actions*, which he hoped would satisfy the Rabbi.

Jesus answered him by telling the story of the good Samaritan. Perhaps you remember the familiar story.

"A Jewish man was traveling on a trip from Jerusalem to Jericho, and he was attacked by bandits. They stripped him of his clothes and money, beat him up, and left him half dead beside the road."

Being a devoted nationalist, no doubt the lawyer's ears would have perked up. The victim of this story was a Jew, one of his own people.

"By chance a Jewish priest came along; but when he saw the man lying there, he crossed to the other side of the road and passed him by."

Can't you envision the looks on the faces of the people listening to Jesus? Priests were supposed to be professional good-deed doers. But in this story, the priest *avoided* the helpless man. If anyone should have known his job description was more about *doing* than teaching and believing, it was a priest.

"A Temple assistant walked over and looked at him lying there," Jesus continued, "but he also passed by on the other side."

The priest ignoring a bleeding man, well, that was shock enough. But a Temple assistant? Here was a Levite, stepping aside. Since the days of Moses, all Levites had been set aside to do the work of the church. Someone with a Levite's pedigree snubbing the injured man would have been scandalous.

For fifteen hundred years, the Levites' assignment was to be the special guardians of the tabernacle and the temple. The priest, who had come upon the man first, had other assignments—offering sacrifices, leading the people in worship, protecting the law. But the Levite's *only* job was to serve wherever he could. And even he looked the other way.

"Then a despised Samaritan came along," Jesus said, "and when he saw the man, he felt deep pity. Kneeling beside him, the Samaritan soothed his wounds with medicine and bandaged them. Then he put the man on his own donkey and took him to an inn, where he took care of him. The next day he handed the innkeeper two pieces of silver and told him to take care of the man. 'If his bill runs higher than that,' he said, 'I'll pay the difference the next time I am here.'"

The lawyer must have hated this part. No group of people was more despised by Jews than the half-breed Samaritans. Making the hero of the story a person of this detestable race would have been repulsive.

It's this simple. Our faith is not saving faith unless it is evidenced by our lifestyle, by what we say and do.

Then Jesus looked straight at the lawyer and asked him a penetrating question.

"Now which one of these three would you say was a neighbor to the man who was attacked by bandits?"

Can't you see the lawyer's face flush with embarrassment? Many in the crowd must have known that his claims to be a devout man were not matched by his actions. His answer would mercilessly expose him, but he had no choice.

"The Samaritan," he seethed. He knew it was *only* the Samaritan who had shown mercy to the bloodied traveler.

"Yes, you're right," Jesus said to the man. "Now *you* go and do what the Samaritan did."

Game. Set. Match.

It's this simple. Our faith is not saving faith unless it is evidenced by our lifestyle, by what we say *and* do.

Treading on Thin Ice

In the eyes of some who are far more astute and formally trained in doctrine and theology, I know I could be treading on thin ice. I'm not saying that our salvation hangs on a thread—to change the metaphor—of goodness and obedience, and if we sin it breaks. But I do believe that the story of the good Samaritan and the misguided lawyer reveals the heart conditions of these men. It clearly confirms the need for seamless continuity between belief and action. What we believe must manifest in what we do. There's nothing in our intellect that will substitute for our obedience.

Confusion About Careers

The years I spent in youth work were enlightening.

One evening a small group of high school seniors sat on our living-room floor. We were discussing leaving home for college, careers, and life choices.

"What do you think you'd like to pursue as a career?" I asked.

"Lawyer," "Doctor," "Teacher," "Scientist," "Entrepreneur," they said, one at a time. One boy said, "Fireman, of course," the answer he's been giving since he was a tyke. We all laughed.

"Okay," I said, "those are good choices. But are there any careers that you could *not* choose because you're a Christian?"

That was a question they hadn't considered, so it took a little while before they spoke.

"Prostitute," one girl answered.

"Mafia boss," a boy said.

"Criminal lawyer," said one outspoken young man.

"*Criminal lawyer?*" I repeated, surprise evident in my voice.

The boy explained that it seemed to him that some criminal lawyers are more interested in winning cases than uncovering the truth. "As a Christian, I don't think I could do that," he concluded.

His comment sparked some lively conversation.

It was a memorable night, for sure, but I have wished many times that I could go back to that evening. I would ask one more question.

"Is there a career that, as a Christian, you *should* take?"

I'm sure there would have been some pained stares as the teens wondered whether I would discourage other marketplace choices. No doubt the obligatory "missionary" or "minister" would have been mentioned.

After their answers died down, my next statement may have shocked them: "As a Christian you really don't have a choice." Then, in this imaginary scene, I would have added a dramatic pause to make sure I had their full attention.

"There's only one choice for a Christian career," I would conclude. "You are all going to have to become priests."

I can just see the shock on their faces. But I wouldn't have left them hanging there very long.

One of the tragedies of religion is that a wall is often created between the secular and the sacred, carrying with it the inherent danger of thinking the "balanced life" includes some activities that are "religious" and others that are "nonreligious." The same is true of art, music, literature, and vocation.

Hundreds of years ago, there was no distinction between secular art and sacred art—only good art and bad art. Incorporating biblical themes into "secular" paintings was not only common but predictable. A visit to any notable art museum plainly reveals masterpieces depicting detailed scenes from the Bible. These works are hung right alongside exquisite portraits and paintings of landscapes and scenes of everyday life.

There was also no division between secular and sacred music. Listening to the classics confirms it.

In literature, the distinction was not between secular and religious writing, but between true and not-true . . . good and bad.

Today in the arts the distinction between religious and nonreligious is clear and strong. Da Vinci, Beethoven, and Dante would have found separate "Christian Contemporary Music Top 40 Charts" and "Christian Best-Seller Lists" to be unnecessary.

Yet in our careers, we have drawn a disturbing line between secular work and "full-time Christian" work.

The New Testament apostles would not have approved.

"You are a chosen people," the apostle Peter wrote to ordinary folks, including painters, musicians, writers, bricklayers, doctors, farmers, teachers, and ministers, "a royal priesthood, a holy nation, a people belonging to God, that you may declare the praises of him who called you out of darkness into his wonderful light."[11]

First-century folks reading these words may have been as shocked as those high school seniors in our living room. But Peter was unequivocal. "You are a full-time professional priest, regardless of your vocation." What that means is that you and I, as people of faith, are *always* people of faith regardless of where we are or what we do. We're always on call. When the person who works next to you loses his job, you're the priest on call. When someone has a flat tire in the parking lot, I'm the priest on call. When our kid's friend gets pregnant, when the neighbor's lawn is overgrown because he's visiting a sick relative out of town, when our pastor calls for volunteers to help with the children, we're the priests on call.

And when tragedy hits people who have thoroughly integrated faith and works, they don't panic and collapse in despair. People of faith know who they are: priests on call.

Faith and Works Revisited

What I love about the verses following Peter's announcement that we are all priests is that he echoes both James and Paul. What we believe must be verified, confirmed, and demonstrated by what we do.

"Once you were not a people," Peter wrote, "but now you are the people of God; once you had not received mercy, but now you have received mercy." *There's* the faith part. And notice that he makes it clear that the people have received this as a gift.

"Live such good lives among the pagans," he goes on, "that, though they accuse you of doing wrong, they may see your good deeds and glorify God on the day he visits us." What we believe and how we act are completely bound together. We cannot work our way to saving faith. But if we're going to have it, it *must be obvious* by our words and deeds. Otherwise it's a sham.

Now, it's critical that the connection between faith and works *not* become ammunition for judging others. Jesus was very clear about the temptation we may have to examine people besides ourselves.

> Judge not, that you be not judged. For with what judgment you judge, you will be judged; and with the measure you use, it will be measured back to you. And why do you look at the speck in your brother's eye, but do not consider the plank in your own eye? Or how can you say to your brother, "Let me remove the speck from your eye"; and look, a plank is in your own eye? Hypocrite! First remove the plank from your own eye, and then you will see clearly to remove the speck from your brother's eye.[12]

This link between faith and works should never create uncertainty about God's ongoing promise of grace in our lives. His promise to save us is sure. "For I am persuaded," the apostle Paul wrote, "that neither death nor life, nor angels nor principalities nor powers, nor things present nor things to come, nor height nor depth, nor any other created thing, shall be able to separate us from the love of God which is in Christ Jesus our Lord."[13]

Like the exclusive and unconditional love espoused in wedding vows, God's love is forever and compels us to respond in obedience. And we *want* our conduct to match the love we promise.

Before All Hell Breaks Loose?

What's interesting about the issue regarding the bond of beliefs and works is that it sounds so philosophical. So otherworldly.

"It's nice to have something like this nailed down," someone might say. "But in real life, what does it look like?" As I mentioned at the beginning of this chapter, the idea of the oneness of belief and works may not sound like a huge idea.

But it is. As Christ-followers—priests on call—we're ready. Like our city's early responders, who never know the moment when they'll be summoned, our guard is never down. At a moment's notice, we can spring into action when the phone call comes, when the news on TV is terrifying—when there seems to be nowhere to turn.

We're called to full-time duty to unite what we believe and how we behave.

"What this means is that those who become Christians become new persons. They are not the same anymore, for the old life is gone. A new life has begun!"[14]

What we believe absolutely impacts how we act. Our interior convictions are confirmed by our exterior conduct. As Christ-followers, we're called to be transformed from the inside out. And this affects everything—when life is humming along smoothly, or when all hell breaks loose.

Setting the Nail

Politics—especially presidential politics—have always fascinated me. My wife points out that one of my greatest disciplinary challenges is turning off 24/7 cable news. It's true.

In 1988, as Ronald Reagan's second term was winding down, there was a scramble in the Republican Party to find a nominee to run for the presidential election and succeed him. Naturally, as the sitting vice president, George H. W. Bush was the immediate front-runner. But there were others.

One of these challengers was an outspoken Christian.

One evening, as I watched a panel discussion among network journalists, one of the commentators made an interesting observation. The subject turned to the candidates' religious beliefs, when the pundit pointed his words toward the Christian candidate. Though every front-runner had in his own way identified himself as a religious person, this particular candidate expressed himself strongly. The commentator spoke with no attempt to mask his disdain about the fact that a presidential candidate called himself a "biblical believer."

Citing a speech the candidate had made, the journalist was very critical. He reminded the other panelists that the Christian, though he acknowledged that he would follow his constitutional responsibility to be the president of *all* the people, had announced that he would not abandon his faith if elected to the White House. His faith would mark every decision.

There was laughter in the booth. Jokes about creating an American theocracy were thrown back and forth. Clearly these reporters believed that a man's beliefs and his works—his actions and decisions—could live in two separate worlds.

Did these commentators know this wasn't the first time that a president—or presidential candidate—had spoken words that connected the responsibility of his call to the sovereignty of God?

Listen to the words of George Washington, America's first president.

In obedience to the public summons, repaired to the present station, it would be peculiarly improper to omit in this first official act my fervent supplications to that Almighty Being who rules over the universe, who presides in the councils of nations, and whose providential aids can supply every human defect, that His benediction may consecrate to the liberties and happiness of the people of the United States.[15]

Our beliefs and our behavior cannot be filed in separate compartments. We're full-time priests—on call—who *happen* to conduct other business—

even presidential business. What we believe and how we act are one. We remember that our assignment is straightforward and clear.

"Whatever you do, do all to the glory of God."[16]

"All" is *all*.

THE SEVENTH THING
TO HAVE NAILED DOWN:
The Church Is God's Idea

Does it surprise you that the final thing to nail down before all hell breaks loose involves the church?

"Certainly," you might say, "if we are only going to nail down seven things, isn't there something more important than an essential about the church? Aren't modern Christ-followers coming up with alternatives that aren't as cumbersome? Is the church relevant any more?"

Let's take a look.

From the Ground Up

Construction has always been one of my personal passions. This was born the summer after my high school graduation, when I landed what was for me a dream job. Jim Whitmer was one of my closest friends, and his father owned a small construction business. Jim had told me, in no uncertain terms, that he had no interest in construction work anymore. His dad told him that if he could find someone to replace him, he'd be off the hook.

I was that someone, and in no time at all, I fell in love with the business.

Richard Whitmer & Sons built custom homes and small commercial structures, but the company's specialty was churches. Because Richard was an enthusiastic Christian, this was an ideal way for him to serve the Lord, building what he happily called "church houses."

So for three summers I joined Richard Whitmer & Sons and helped to build custom homes, commercial structures, and churches.

Before learning the business, I thought churches were constructed on top of the clay layer of earth just a few feet below the surface.[1]

But I was wrong. Churches are not built on top of clay.

This Thing Called "the Church"

Remember the getaway in Caesarea Philippi, where the Savior asked His followers what people were saying about Him? And remember all of their responses (Elijah, Jeremiah, John the Baptist), and how Jesus then asked them, "But who do *you* think I am?"?

You remember that Simon Peter was quick to answer. "You're the Christ, the Messiah," he announced, "the Son of the Living God."

Jesus congratulated Peter but told him that he hadn't come up with this profound truth on his own; God Himself had disclosed it to him.

And then Jesus used a new word, one the disciples may have never heard before. At least, this is the first time we see it in our Bibles. "You are [*Petros*]," Jesus tells Peter, "and on this rock I will build My church, and the gates of [Hell] shall not prevail against it."[2]

The new word was *church*. Don't you think the disciples must have looked puzzled when Jesus said it?

Church? they must have wondered. *What's that?*

Church meant "called-out ones," and not only did the disciples soon learn what Jesus was talking about, but they eventually spread out as far away as India to build them.[3] Most of them died in the process of establishing this thing called the church.

Of course, Jesus was not telling the disciples that the church's actual foundation would be built on the man Peter. It was to be built on the *truth* that Peter had just spoken about Jesus.

"You are the Messiah," Peter had said.

"On *this* rock, I'll build My church," Jesus had responded.

Previously, as Jesus and the twelve disciples were traveling to the region of Caesarea Philippi, they had walked through the Hulah Valley, near the mouth of a cave known as "the Gates of Hell," from which flowed one of the largest springs that supplied water to the Jordan River.[4]

In the disciples' minds was the image of water pouring out of this cave toward the Jordan. "It will be as impossible for the power of hell itself to hold back the church as for you to try to hold back the water gushing from that cave," Jesus was saying.

The imagery would have been poignant—and confusing—to the disciples. They had no idea what Jesus was talking about. How could anything hold back those forceful waters?

The disciples' apprehension is understandable. For centuries God's people had been persecuted and maligned. Conquerors had plundered and scattered the Jews, making fugitives and exiles out of them. At that time their land was occupied by the indomitable Romans. And they witnessed paralyzing infighting and conflict between the religious elites and the commoners. The disciples wondered how Jesus could build something strong enough to hold back the evil they saw all around. They felt powerless. The whole concept seemed outlandish.

But as hope burns when ignited by inspired ideas, their resolve quickened at the possibility of such a thing. Today, with history as our teacher, you and I know what Jesus was talking about.

The church of Jesus Christ, visible and invisible, has the power to accomplish a lot more than holding back water spouting from a cave. The church can literally stand against the evil schemes of hell itself.

> *The church can literally stand against the evil schemes of hell itself.*

You have heard people say that the church is not a building. That's true. As the book of Hebrews describes it, with Christ as the "High Priest," the church is a "more perfect tabernacle not made with hands."[5]

But in addition to being the worldwide collection of Christ-followers, the church is, in fact, a building standing on a piece of land.

God Is Into Real Estate

Every contractor knows that without available land, there is no place for him to ply his craft. Without dirt he's out of business. God had a plan to build the church, and He started by picking out a strategic piece of property.

About two thousand years before Jesus introduced the word *church* to His disciples, God stirred the heart of a man named Terah to leave his homeland in Ur of the Chaldeans. Ur was located near the area known as the Fertile Crescent, the place where the Tigris and Euphrates Rivers meet just northwest of the Persian Gulf.

Terah moved and took his son, his son's wife, and his grandson to a place called Haran. It was a journey of about four hundred miles. After a few years in Haran, Terah died. Then God spoke to Abram, Terah's son.

> Now the LORD . . . said to Abram: "Get out of your country, from your family and from your father's house, to a land that I will show you. I will make you a great nation; I will bless you and make your name great; and you shall be a blessing. I will bless those who bless you, and I will curse him who curses you; and in you all the families of the earth shall be blessed."[6]

God sent Abram to a tract of *land*—real estate—about three hundred miles away. "This is My land, and you are to settle here," He told Abram.

It is amazing that today, four thousand years later, Abram's descendents, the Jews, still lay claim to Canaan, that very same piece of real estate.

When Abram, his wife, Sarai, and his nephew, Lot, arrived in Canaan, there was famine in the land. So they moved on, finally landing in Egypt, where they lived for ten years.

Once the famine was over in Canaan, Abram headed straight back to the land that God had promised to him. There God made a covenant that Abram would become the father of an entire nation.

God's promise of a nation—His chosen people—was passed down through Abram to his son, Isaac, and his grandson, Jacob, the father of twelve sons who established the nation of Israel.[7]

Almost 170 years after the promised heir, Isaac, was born to Abraham and Sarah, Joseph, one of Isaac's grandsons, was sold into slavery by his jealous brothers.[8] Joseph's new owners took him to Egypt, where he was again sold, this time winding up in the house of a prominent Egyptian leader named Potiphar. But God had a plan to build the church.

This continued the odyssey of Israel's children, still in Canaan but facing another crisis of famine. They were forced to pull up stakes and resettle in Egypt. There they lived, first as guests but eventually as slaves. Then, almost three hundred years after Joseph's arrival in Egypt, the Israelites left Egypt and headed back to their homeland. This trip from Egypt to Canaan—the promised land—across the wilderness of the Sinai Peninsula took forty years.

God Enters the Construction Business

Every construction boss's worktable is the hood of his pickup truck. Rolling out the blueprint of the project he's working on a common sight. When God was ready to build the church, He rolled out a plan

On the Israelites' way from Egypt to Canaan, you could say God expanded

His interest from real estate and joined the construction trade. God built a building, or He at least ordered one to be built to His exact specifications. Moses had just come down from the mountain where he had received the Ten Commandments. "Speak to the children of Israel," God told him. "Take up an offering from the people for a special purpose." Then God explained to Moses the reason for this unusual fund-raising campaign. "And let them make Me a sanctuary," God continued, "that I may dwell among them. According to all that I show you, that is, the pattern of the tabernacle and the pattern of all its furnishings, just so you shall make it."[9] God told Moses to build a building so that He could "dwell among them."

That doesn't mean God wasn't around until that time. The Old Testament account makes it clear that God was very present and very visible among the people, as visible as a pillar of cloud by day and a pillar fire by night. But now God wanted to have a visible structure—a dwelling place—that the people could enter into and experience His presence.

A place for sacrifice and worship, the tabernacle would also be the resting place for the ark of the covenant, the gold-inlaid box that contained the Ten Commandments.

This was not a stationary building. Because the Jews were on the move, God's dwelling place had to be collapsible and portable. So the tabernacle was constructed with animal skins and large pieces of linen sewn with goat's hair, and stretched out between poles.

When it was time to move to a new location on their journey to Canaan, the tabernacle could be dismantled and loaded onto carts to be transported. The descendants of Levi, Jacob's third son, were selected to be the tabernacle's teardown/setup crew.

For the Israelites, the tabernacle was a sacred structure. It was their "church."

Almost five hundred years later, the construction of the permanent tabernacle—the temple—was begun in Jerusalem.

The tabernacle had been God's transportable dwelling place in the wilderness. Solomon's temple would be His immovable house in Jerusalem.

It was a thousand years later that Jesus, God's Son, announced He would build another place, *His* church. And today, two thousand years later, the earth is covered with tabernacles—ordinary buildings, great cathedrals, and grass huts. These are dwelling places, where people go to meet with God.

In the Old Testament, God's people were released from bondage in Egypt. They heard directly from God through the giving of the law. As a result, they built the tabernacle, God's dwelling place.

Beginning in the New Testament and continuing today, God's people, through Christ, are also released from bondage, the bondage of sin. They, too, have heard directly from God through His gift of Jesus. As a result, they built the church, God's dwelling place.

In the wilderness the tabernacle was where the Israelites went to meet God. Years later it was the temple in downtown Jerusalem where they went to be in the presence of God. Today, you and I walk inside a church building, and God is there.

Storm Shelters

When a hurricane is on its way, the authorities tell people to flee to buildings strong enough to withstand devastating winds. Usually school gymnasiums or other structures built with concrete block are chosen. Sometimes storm shelters are basements of great buildings. If you haven't actually been inside an evacuation area, you may have at least watched newscasts showing rows of cots set up to accommodate emergency visitors.

Of course, there are always some people who avoid the shelters and weather the storms on their own. In spite of the news bulletins that plead, "Evacuate your homes; find safe shelter," these folks stubbornly ride out the storm, and carnage, alone.

The same devastation can happen when people decide to ride out life without the church.

"I can worship God from my fishing boat," some say. "Actually, being close to nature is better for me than being in church."

"Our lives are so frazzled," others confess, "and a quiet weekend at home is just the same as worship for our family."

Some people may stay away simply because of personal tastes: "Have you heard the music they play? I can't stand it!"

Having raised a family and known the stress of frenetic schedules and overburdened weekday commitments, Bobbie and I understand these conclusions, these rationalizations for skipping church. But it's precisely because of the inevitable coming stress that we need the storm shelter.

> *It's precisely because of the inevitable coming stress that we need the storm shelter.*

Not surprisingly, the Bible weighs in on the importance of showing up at church, this special dwelling place of God. "Let us not neglect our meeting together, as some people do, but encourage and warn each other."[10] Heb. 10:25

As important as it is nail down the critical tenets of our faith—the nature of God, the power of the Bible, the truth of our lostness, the character of Jesus, God's gifts of grace and faith, and the oneness of belief and works—the regular gathering in church with other believers cannot be seen as anything but absolutely essential.

A Great Place to Collapse

Not long ago, our pastor was preparing to invite the children to walk to the front of the church for the "Time for Young Disciples" children's sermon. As he stood at the chancel steps, a man sitting on the front pew leaned forward and collapsed onto the floor in a dead faint.

Though our sanctuary is large and the man's crumbling was not visible to most of us, those close enough to see the man fall out of his seat onto the carpet made enough commotion to create a noticeable stir. What followed in the wake of this unpredicted emergency looked like a perfectly orchestrated exercise.

"We need a doctor's help," Dr. David Swanson, our pastor, announced. His voice reflected no panic at all. Like a cue to ready soldiers, the simple words were a measured call for help. As though they had rehearsed for this, several doctors and nurses quickly made their way to the fallen man. Walter Parks, our head usher, summoned other ushers to bring oxygen and a case filled with medical supplies. Walt then shepherded a wheelchair down the aisle.

Without any prompting, the organist, George Atwell, began to play a familiar hymn. A thousand people sat quietly, many of us praying for the man's health and that God would grant wisdom for those attending to his care.

Our pastor and one of the associate ministers stood close to the man's family, comforting and embracing them. Another associate called 911 on his cell phone.

After a few minutes of watching this flawlessly choreographed response, Bobbie leaned over to me and whispered, "This is a great place to collapse."

About ten minutes later, the man regained consciousness and was lifted onto the waiting wheelchair and pushed out of the sanctuary. Family members followed. Dr. Swanson and the other pastors returned to their places, and the service continued.

Driving home that morning, Bobbie and I talked about the drama. It was a perfect picture of what takes place at church when all hell breaks loose. What we had witnessed when a man physically collapsed is exactly what your local church—the one just down the street from your home—is prepared to do when emotional, physical, or spiritual tragedy strikes you and your family. The church is a great place to collapse.

The visible church—the one with an address, city, state, and zip code—

stands as a ready storm shelter when all hell breaks loose. Riding out any storm on your own doesn't make sense. To fly solo is to take a huge and unnecessary risk.

It was God's plan to build the church.

But there is another "church." One that isn't constructed with brick and mortar.

The Other Church

In the second chapter, we talked about who God is and how He has chosen to reveal Himself in creation. But wouldn't it be great if we could actually *see* Him?

How is that possible today?

In describing the church, the apostle Paul talks about groups of people who gather together to seek and worship God. The physical location of these meetings is unimportant. In fact, the people who meet are a part of a great worldwide fraternity of like-minded believers. Paul names these people, the "body of Christ."

> For as the body is one and has many members, but all the members of that one body, being many, are one body, so also is Christ. For by one Spirit we were all baptized into one body—whether Jews or Greeks, whether slaves or free—and have all been made to drink into one Spirit. For in fact the body is not one member but many. . . . But now indeed there are many members, yet one body. . . . And if one member suffers, all the members suffer with it; or if one member is honored, all the members rejoice with it. Now you are the body of Christ, and members individually.[11]

In this passage, God is announcing, "Do you want to see what I look like? Then look at these people. Notice how they treat one another. This is Me." And it doesn't matter how large or small the gathering. He can even be seen among two or three (Matt. 18:20).

The Church Family

From the time I was a youngster in my dad's church, I heard the expression "the church family." Today I understand what a profound and accurate image this is: a family.

Because of how the church body works, there should be no such thing as a lonely church member. The Greek word for fellowship is *koinonia*, and it means a special kind of connecting.[12]

Nowhere else can you—and every member of your family—find a place where your are simultaneously confronted with the truth, embraced by people who love you, and encouraged to have a life of significance. Talk to people whose lives have been hit by sickness or tragedy. Like the first responders who surrounded the fallen man in our sanctuary, the church body swings into action both at times of celebration and crisis.

"Without the church, what happens when you get sick?" a conference speaker once asked the audience. "What happens when you get married, or have a baby, or lose your job, or *die?*" he added, punctuating the last word. It's God's plan to build the church, for all of these reasons and more.

Under a microscope you would see that your body consists of an amazing network of billions of cells. A close examination of the church body also shows its marvelous and intricate composition.

All around the world, small "accountability" groups of Christians meet. Group members demonstrate their love and genuine affection for one another by asking tough questions. "Does what you're about to do square with the spiritual goals you set for yourself?"

"What's going *on?*"

Sometimes these questions and confrontations save people from devastation. People who encourage and admonish one another are part of the church.

Anyone can take a look at the special "affinity groups" that regularly gather within the church family for instruction, help, and encouragement: mothers of toddlers, blended-family ministries, free car care for single moms, marriage workshops, elder care, mission groups, teen sports teams, men's groups, divorce-recovery care, substance abuse programs, single-parent ministries, grief workshops, adoption support groups, post-abortion trauma assistance, and aid for families dealing with a disability or sexual addiction.

> *A special kind of fellowship takes over when all hell breaks loose for one of its members. That's why God planned the church.*

The church family is there to rejoice and celebrate and support people through every life stage, and it is a safety net when people face tough times. A special kind of fellowship takes over when all hell breaks loose for one of its members. That's why God planned the church.

Stand and Sing

Baseball is "America's favorite pastime." Although the game originated from ball-and-bat activities played in Britain long ago, its current version was developed in the United States. So it's no surprise that every baseball game begins with "The Star-Spangled Banner." What I love about this pregame musical moment is that every fan, regardless of his or her team loyalty, stands, faces the Stars and Stripes, and sings. A flag has been raised that trumps partisanship. The same is true with football games at every level.

On January 27, 1991, the New York Giants and the Buffalo Bills were preparing to play in Super Bowl XXV in Tampa. Exactly ten days earlier,

President George H. W. Bush had, with the approval of Congress, declared war on Saddam Hussein because of his unprovoked invasion of Kuwait. The mood in America was one of fear and palpable anxiety. Since the United States was fully engaged in war—Operation Desert Storm—security at the Tampa stadium was raised to unprecedented levels.

As the football game was about to begin, Whitney Houston stepped to the microphone and began to sing the national anthem.[13] For the next three minutes, there were no New York Giants fans in America. No Buffalo Bills fans. There were only Americans. Everyone in the stadium was standing in solidarity. And most of them were singing.

In the same way, the church is a place for camaraderie. For standing and singing, for worship and celebration. It's the place where people set aside those things that often separate them.

The children's song wafting from a church classroom filled with little ones wraps this colorful truth in a tidy bundle. "Red and yellow, black and white, all are precious in His sight."[14]

The church was designed by God to be the gathering place for people who love Jesus Christ. The place where they mutually align themselves with Him. Then all partisanship and bickering and divisions can be eliminated. It was God's plan to build the church.

Get Me to the Woodshed on Time

What would life be like without discipline? Like a river that overflows its banks and becomes a festering swamp, a world without authority and order would be chaos. Shoplifters would go unapprehended. Reckless drivers would speed through quiet neighborhoods. Predators of every description would victimize the weak. That's why civil governments were put in place. To provide protection for the innocent and punishment for society's offenders.

But what brings unrepentant, immoral people to account?

If you've never thought of the church in this role, a look back through history reveals that one of her most important reasons for existence has been to exercise moral authority. This authority was never intended to be used in haughtiness or for revenge. But church discipline has been administered to correct its misguided, harmful, or defiantly unrepentant members, protecting the purity of the church body.

In matters of church discipline, Paul makes no play for diplomacy with the first-century church in Corinth:

> I can hardly believe the report about the sexual immorality going on among you, something so evil that even the pagans don't do it. I am told that you have a man in your church who is living in sin with his father's wife. And you are so proud of yourselves! Why aren't you mourning in sorrow and shame? And why haven't you removed this man from your fellowship? . . . Don't you realize that if even one person is allowed to go on sinning, soon all will be affected? . . . It isn't my responsibility to judge outsiders, but it certainly is your job to judge those inside the church who are sinning in these ways. God will judge those on the outside; but as the Scriptures say, "You must remove the evil person from among you."[15]

When Bobbie and I moved to Florida, we bought a home in a small community governed by covenants and bylaws. With complete legal authority, our homeowners association has the right to hold neighbors accountable for disobeying what's written in these documents. When homeowners refuse to comply—like not paying their annual dues—power is given to the association to place liens and even sell the offender's house on the courthouse steps. Homeowners associations rarely take their power to this extreme, but the right to use their authority is clearly theirs.

In the same way, God gives the church the authority to discipline "brothers and sisters" whose actions and attitudes conflict with Scripture.

In addition to the biblical instructions, many churches and denominations have specific, written procedures to ensure that offenses are confronted with precision and care.

The ultimate goal of church discipline is not to destroy a person. It's to so radically challenge him that he repents and is restored to fellowship in the church. And like a good parent, the right to discipline is balanced with the mandate to love and serve.

A Launching Pad for Servants

In the fall of 2005, a category 4 hurricane slammed into the Gulf Coast. Six months after Katrina made landfall, drowning New Orleans and other cities along the coast, the Associated Press released a feature story that was published in newspapers across America. One paragraph read, "With government agencies stretched thin by the massive scope of the Gulf Coast recovery effort, groups from every conceivable religious denomination are shouldering a heavy share of the workload. Tens of thousands of volunteers from hundreds of faith-based groups have poured into the region."[16]

Another paragraph made a statement about the resources of the church that would have made Jesus' first disciples smile: "That virtually bottomless well of labor makes [these church groups] a valuable resource for the Federal Emergency Management Agency, which coordinates their efforts to avoid duplication."[17]

How fantastic is that? The church's response to one of American history's most devastating disasters was so comprehensive that a federal agency had to make sure that in their zeal, Christian volunteer groups didn't duplicate the efforts of paid government agencies.

From hurricane disaster relief, to feeding hot lunches to shut-ins, to taking healing to millions of AIDS-racked Africans, to airlifting food and medical supplies to drought-stricken regions, to caring for the homeless, the church has picked up the towel and basin and shovel and soup ladle and chainsaw and medicine kit . . . and has faithfully served. It was God's plan to build the church.

A Stronghold Against Evil

We've talked about how the church is a storm shelter, a structure that's certified to withstand storms of every kind. A building filled with faithful people. This is true, but there's more.

As steadfast as the church is during whatever calamity may befall our lives, it's even stronger than we imagine. Jesus declared to His disciples that the church is strong enough to hold back the power of Satan himself.

The church is actually designed for warfare. In addition to having buildings where the church family meets—where there's instruction, celebration, and discipline, and where servants are unleashed—the church boasts a military initiative of unrivaled power.

Like outposts guarding the vulnerable open shorelines against marauding predators, churches are fortresses lining the streets of your town, empowered to hold off the power of darkness. And like a member of our own intelligence force that penetrate the rival camp and report back to headquarters, the apostle Paul tells us about the awful archenemies of the church. "We are not fighting against people made of flesh and blood, but against the evil rulers and authorities of the unseen world, against those mighty powers of darkness who rule this world, and against wicked spirits in the heavenly realms."[18]

When Jesus said that the "gates of hell" would not be able to hold up against the strength of His church, He was talking about these unseen enemies, headed by their crafty general, Satan.

Satan hates the church. It stands for everything he despises. And it's his goal to keep people away—to isolate them and render them defenseless.

But if the enemy is unsuccessful at keeping believers from meeting together, then he'll do everything in his power to destroy the church body from the inside. He'll put people at odds with one another over the authority of God's Word or the church's historic tenets, or to drain the people's energy with arguments over music styles or the color of the carpet.

The church poses such a threat to his evil schemes. Anything Satan can do to break down the stronghold, he'll do. But the church is equipped to overcome the evil one.

Never on Sunday

Several years ago some friends of ours found their "dream home on a lake" and moved. But their new home was farther from their church, and they decided it was a hassle to keep attending.

After several months in their beautiful new home, they began a casual search for a new church. But soon they gave up, knowing that it could never replace the church they had left. Consciously or not, by forsaking their search, they made the decision that they no longer needed the church.

Our friends thought that they could ride out the storm alone. They were wrong. Because they were isolated from friends who loved them, no one close by saw what was happening or really cared.

Their marriage began to unravel. Their children grew distant. Open communication within their home ground to a halt. Soon unresolved issues bubbled to the surface. Uncontrolled rage surfaced. Divorce lawyers were summoned. All hell broke loose. These friends hadn't gone to the storm shelter.

Without a church family, without a constant hearing of the truth, without a place to celebrate, without the voices of loving friends to call us to account, without the chance to serve, and without the protection that Jesus promised against "the gates of hell," we are left vulnerable. That's why the stronghold—the tabernacle, the temple, the church—stands. It's God's plan.

Miracles Happen at Church

Our friend Dr. Henry Blackaby says, "Miracles happen at church." He's right. Someone at church may be the answer to my prayer. Something I say in a conversation may be the very thing someone else is looking for. An idea or a solution for something you need this week may come to your mind while sitting in worship.

Several months ago, Bobbie called Molly, an old friend in Virginia, and in the course of the conversation asked, "Where are you going to church?"

Caring for her aging father after her mother had died complicated Molly's life and she hadn't been to church for over a year.

"Well, now I know the reason I was supposed to call you," Bobbie joked. "You need to be in church, Molly. It's where Jesus went on the Sabbath, and He's still there every Sunday. You need to go to church."

As challenging as it was, Molly made arrangements so she could attend church the next week. A few days later, Bobbie received an envelope in the mail from her friend. Folded inside the envelope was the church bulletin—the program—from the service she had attended.

Written in the bulletin's margins were notes that Molly had taken during the service.

The music and the sermon had been just what Molly needed. The letter she wrote was filled with celebration and gratitude. Molly had experienced the miracle.

"I went to church today," Molly wrote. "It was a service that felt complete. I don't know how else to describe it. Thank you for reminding me to jump-start my spiritual battery."

One visit to the tabernacle, surrounded by the body of Christ, and we can experience the dwelling place of our heavenly Father. *This* is God's plan for the church.

Home Base

The other day, as I was walking our dog, I saw some of the neighborhood kids playing hide-and-seek. It was fun watching them and remembering the hours my brothers and I spent as kids playing the same game. During the years we spent in Japan, where our parents were missionaries, we learned an Asian rendition of hide-and-seek called "kick-the-can."

The liability of being "it" in this game is that it's you versus dozens of neighbor kids. The chances of prevailing are zero. When you are "it," you are basically "it" for the duration.

One of the common features of hide-and-seek and kick-the-can was "home base." If you got there before being tagged, you were safe.

When you and I walk into church, we should experience the same emotion kids feel when they touch home base. We're safe.

That doesn't mean the church is all fun and games. It's not. Truth can be tough on us. Church is a place where we're confronted and lovingly challenged to the hard work of confessing our sin and renewing our resolve to obedience. But the church—visible and invisible—is the place where God dwells. It's a place for community and celebration and service. It's a place of refuge from Satan's terrorism. It's a place for miracles.

Setting the Nail

If you've ever visited the northern coast of England, you know about the ocean squalls that often ravage that area. Late in the nineteenth century, English pastor Vernon J. Charlesworth wrote a poem that became a great old hymn, often sung by fisherman as they headed for shore during a storm.

The Lord's our Rock, in Him we hide,
A Shelter in the time of storm;
Secure whatever ill betide,
A Shelter in the time of storm.
Oh, Jesus is a Rock in a weary land,
A weary land, a weary land;
Oh, Jesus is a Rock in a weary land,
A shelter in the time of storm.[19]

Just as He said it would be, the church is built on the Rock of Jesus Christ. There's nothing quite like the church, and it's *exactly* where you and I need to be before, during, and after all hell breaks loose.

9

SWEATERS, STORM SHUTTERS, AND BEING READY

We don't have winter in Florida, at least not the kind I experienced as a kid growing up in Chicago. When Bobbie and I moved south in 2000, some of our northern friends asked us, "Won't you miss the seasons?"

"Oh, we'll have seasons," we said. "We'll travel to them."

And we do. Because of family and business, between September and March we can actually wear wool coats and enjoy snow when we travel north.

Packing is interesting. With air conditioning at full blast in our home and walking around in shorts and T-shirts, we're putting turtlenecks, sweaters, and heavy coats into our suitcases. It's strange to be packing clothing so diametrically unlike what we need at the moment. But the idea of showing up in subzero weather wearing flip-flops and a swimsuit would be ridiculous. So we plan ahead.

And Shutters on the Windows

When hurricanes battered our state in 2004, plywood was a hot commodity. People by the dozens were driving to Home Depot and Lowe's for four-by-eight plywood sheets, stacking them on top of their cars. We weren't ready for the first storm. But as the second one approached, we visited Home Depot too, buying plywood to cover one of our outside windows. This second-story window that faces east was the most vulnerable. Given the way it trembled during the heaviest gusts of wind in the first storm, we were surprised—and very glad—that it hadn't shattered.

So we bought the plywood. During the installation adventure, I realized that hoisting a big sheet of plywood up a ladder and screwing it to the house was not going to be easy. The wind doesn't know the difference between a piece of plywood twenty feet in the air and a sail.

We need permanent storm shutters for this window, I thought to myself.

So as soon as I had my temporary solution in place, I went to my computer and began looking for local companies that featured storm shutters. Bobbie helped in the search.

But after calling three or four storm-shutter companies, it didn't take us long to realize that in the middle of hurricane season we weren't the only people with this idea.

"Because of the high demand for our products, we're not able to take any new orders," one phone message said. Another clicked to an electronic messaging system announcing, "The voice mailbox you are trying to reach is full." The last company we tried never even picked up the phone. After ten or twelve rings, we hung up. Plywood would have to do.

Four months later, after hurricane season was in the history books, we decided to see again if we could buy storm shutters for that east-facing, second-story window.

You know where this is going, don't you?

"Hello. Central Florida Shutter Company. How can we help you?" the friendly voice said after the second ring.

The salesman was at our house two days later, measuring our upstairs window. He offered "a substantial discount, if you order today."

Just months earlier, we couldn't get anyone to even answer their phones. Now we were being offered a discount.

The day the installation crew came, the sky was crystal clear and the breeze was almost indiscernible. Installing storm shutters in perfect weather looked really funny.

But it's not. It's the right thing to do.

In the same way that packing sweaters in hot weather and mounting storm shutters in March are counterintuitive, nailing the seven things down when life is good may not feel important. It is.

When you step off the plane in Chicago on a winter day, you'd better have your coat on. When the hurricanes come, the storm shutters need to be securely on that window. And when crisis hits, what you have stored away in your heart is all that you will be able to pull up at that moment.

It's Easier to Build on Sand

Our sixteen years of living in Nashville were wonderful. We made lifelong friends and enjoyed the beautiful topography of the area. The gently rolling hills painted a lovely backdrop. But sometimes the traffic got a little snarled, especially when the highway department decided to improve the roads.

Widening a road by a lane or two meant years of frustrating delays. Why? Because those pretty hills were solid limestone. Dynamite and heavy-duty equipment were the only ways to blast through them.

In sandy and flat Florida, building a new road is just a matter of cutting

> *The time to build is right now, before the rain and winds arrive.*

the palmettos and brush away and pouring concrete. It takes a month or two.

In Tennessee, when the torrential rains come, the roads aren't fazed. But in Florida, washouts and sinkholes are so common that they hardly make the news. So, even though it's much easier to build stuff on sand, it's worth the extra effort to look around for some rock on which to do your building.

Believe it or not, Jesus talked about this.

Everyone who hears my words and obeys them is like a wise man who built his house on rock. It rained hard, the floods came, and the winds blew and hit that house. But it did not fall, because it was built on rock. Everyone who hears my words and does not obey them is like a foolish man who built his house on sand. It rained hard, the floods came, and the winds blew and hit that house, and it fell with a big crash.[1]

Even if the construction process is more time-consuming and challenging, the essentials must be nailed down on rock, not sand. And the time to build is right now, before the rain and winds arrive.

> My hope is built on nothing less
> Than Jesus' blood and righteousness.
> I dare not trust the sweetest frame,
> But wholly lean on Jesus' name.
>
> His oath, His covenant, His blood,
> Support me in the whelming flood.
> When all around my soul gives way,
> He then is all my Hope and Stay.

On Christ the solid rock I stand,
All other ground is sinking sand.[2]

How Hell Breaks Loose

When all hell breaks loose, it can happen in different ways. What has come to mind as you've reflected on your own difficult experiences or those of your friends? Let's take a look again at some of the things that may bring on the devastation we call, "Hell breaking loose."

It can happen because of . . .

A Foolish Choice We Make

There are times when the trauma we're facing is a direct result of something we have done or failed to do.

The biblical account of the young runaway who told his father that he wished he were dead, then defiantly traveled to a faraway country and wasted his money, is the story of someone who's in trouble because his choices *put* him there.

He brought it on himself.

But hell can also break loose because of . . .

A Foolish Choice Someone Else Makes

Some folks who are looking down the gun barrel of "hell breaking loose" are victims. Several years ago, a woman sat in our living room pouring out to Bobbie her painful story of childhood physical and emotional abuse. Her father had cashed in his superior strength and power, devastating his little girl for his own pleasure. And though it had happened decades earlier, the scars still felt fresh.

Her tragic story reminds me of the lost coin in the Bible.[3] Coins do not have the will or the capability to get lost. They don't crawl away to some undisclosed location under their own power. But because of the negligence of their owners, they can be misplaced. Their dilemma is not their own doing.

Then, hell can break loose because of . . .

An Unplanned Tragedy

Every time we open the morning paper or log on to our favorite news Web site, stories of devastation and tragedy shout to us. "Tornadoes Rip Through Midwest, 15 Dead." "School Principal Shot." "Mideast Violence Escalates." "Terrorist Plot Uncovered."

Sometimes the newspaper isn't the only source of fear. You are stricken with a life-threatening illness. Your friends' child is seriously injured in an automobile accident. Your house is burglarized, and valuables are missing.

People who are the recipients of a doctor's bad report, or who happen to be in the crosshairs of a wayward oncoming car or who are a target for thieves probably did not make foolish choices. But the hell they face is no less striking.

Blowing out your knee in a backyard basketball game or waking in the middle of the night with a kidney-stone attack, or receiving the surprise news of a lost loved one could also fit into this "innocent victim" category.

Jesus told a story of a farmer who lost one of his sheep. Unlike the lost boy, whose insubordination got him in trouble, or the lost coin, misplaced by someone else's carelessness, the sheep wandered off innocently. A bite of grass here, another, more appealing mouthful over there, and still another *way* over there . . . and pretty soon the sheep was missing in action. The sheep was neither defiant nor a victim, but it was in serious trouble nonetheless. In fact, it was in perilous straits. If it hadn't been for the farmer's timely rescue, this lamb surely would have been torn apart by a hungry predator.

Things in Your Past

Sometimes it's helpful to identify the reason for the crisis you are facing. Recognizing the root cause can be very useful. But as tempting as it is to spend time analyzing the whys and wherefores of our moments of tragedy, there is danger in getting stuck there. Dwelling on something in the past that we cannot control or change is counterproductive. The "if onlys" of our foolish choices or the acrimony toward those who victimized us will not provide any help with what you and I are facing right now. And grousing about our predicament or touting our innocence doesn't transform us.

Someone has wisely said that it doesn't matter what happens to us; it's what *happens* to what happens to us that really matters. The origin of the tragedy—the reason for hell breaking loose—may be interesting to talk about over coffee with your closest friend. But what you and I *do* at the moment when hell breaks loose is what matters.

The apostle Paul settles the issue of looking back. By his own example, he encourages us to not remember . . . to lose our memories: "Forgetting those things which are behind and reaching forward to those things which are ahead, I press toward the goal for the prize of the upward call of God in Christ Jesus."[4]

Reading this, it's tempting to call Paul an out-of-touch idealist. He's not, because he precedes his counsel with this: "I do not regard myself as having laid hold of it yet; but one thing I do . . ."[5]

Predictably, this determination to not look back and dwell on the past is a challenging one. It's tough to let go of bitterness or regret. Yet what does Paul decide? He decides to *do* something: "this thing I *do*!" I *will* forget the past.

When all hell breaks loose, it peels back the cover to reveal exactly who we are. C. S. Lewis said, "Surely what a man does when he is taken off his guard is the best evidence for what sort of man he is."[6] Further, who he is, is

My level of future success when all hell breaks loose depends on one thing: how well I prepare for it right now, long before the devastation arrives.

the accumulation of what he knows and believes. And what he knows and believes comes from his own relentless pursuit of truth.

My level of future success when all hell breaks loose depends on one thing: how well I prepare for it *right now*, long before the devastation arrives. Collecting and knowing the essentials—nailing them down—is a game plan that can prepare us for anything. It is something we can *do*.

Addressing the seven things that we must have nailed before hell breaks loose, I have sought to provide a biblically based foundation for truth. Of course, we have only scratched the surface. It's only a start . . . but it *is* a start.

When the moment comes—and it *will* come for you and for me—when the unexpected arrives and your heart pounds with indescribable panic, the seven things you have nailed down will provide solace and confidence. Like a steel beam under a heavy load, these rock-solid biblical truths will sustain you. Having built a godly interior life will have been the *best* preparation.

Let's take a few minutes and review.

#1 God Is God

The truth God delivered from the burning bush to an insecure and fearful Moses is still true right now. "I AM who I AM," God said. "And," He could have added, "you're not."

Like the security a child feels as she reaches up for her father's hand, the assurance that we are not alone is a gift from the great "I AM." He is here, and He is in charge.

On September 11, 2001, between 8:45 in the morning—the moment that American Airlines Flight 11 slammed into the north tower of the World Trade Center—and 10:28, when that tower cascaded to the ground, multiple phone calls to and from family members and close friends were estimated in the billions.[7] Trunk lines around the world were challenged to their full capacity.

"Are you there?" people said to each another. "I just want to hear your voice." And though airports were closed to any commercial travel, millions of Americans anxious to connect with their loved ones found ways to get home.

In tragic times, the fact that God is God provides us with more sanctuary than we can imagine, and it's just what we need.

Like a parent watching a child on the playground, God is always looking after us with a loving eye. He is God.

"God is our refuge and strength, always ready to help in times of trouble. So we will not fear, even if earthquakes come and the mountains crumble into the sea."[8] Psalm 46:1-2

God Is the Creator

It's great assurance to you and me—when tragedy strikes—that God made us. "We are His workmanship," Paul tells us.[9] He could have added, "There's nothing about us that He doesn't know and love."

The book you're holding right now is a "made thing." As you sit reading it, there will never be a moment of doubt that *someone* printed its pages and bound them into a book. If you look up from this page, you'll see more "made things." Fabrics, furniture, light fixtures. Someone trying to convince you that any of these just appeared without a designer and builder would make you laugh.

You and I are "made things" too. Our eyes, our limbs, our internal organs were custom-built, made to order by God. He knows all about us physically.

Not only did He create our physiques, but God also designed our emotions.

The joy and satisfaction we feel, as well as anxiety and anger and panic, He understands. Not a single feeling that you and I experience surprises Him. He made us.

And not only did He make you and me, but the vastness of the universe is also God's creation, set in place by His command. The brilliance of the sunset and the panoply of stars that follow, hawks that circle overhead without flapping their wings, and the delicate petals of the wildflowers in the field across from your house—all of these are His doing.

God Is Holy

Although words like *perfect* and *clean* and *set apart* may help us envision what "holy" means, they still fall short. God's holiness, His faultlessness, is a mystery that cannot be fully explained or comprehended.

It was God's holiness that overwhelmed men and women in the Bible, sending them to the ground on their faces in His breathtaking presence.

Imagine how you or I would feel if we walked into the kitchen early tomorrow morning and Jesus Christ was sitting at the table, slowly stirring a fresh cup of tea and waiting for us. We would be speechless. Overwhelmed. The experience of seeing His magnificence would be more than we could take. The Bible is filled with stories of people who were overcome simply by being in God's holy presence.

Our culture loves superlatives. Dozens of cities, it seems, boast the world's largest shopping mall. Superior athletes in every major sport are often postulated by the pundits as "perhaps the best in his/her sport in history." And some major hospitals purport to be "the best in the country" when referring to their medical staff. We love superlatives.

When trouble comes, a holy God is the most qualified specialist in the cosmos. His perfection is sure. Knowing His character and relying on who His is when crisis comes brings inexpressible security. He is eternity's best. No one—no *thing*—is His equal. God is holy.

God Is Sovereign

God is active and participates in His creation, twenty-four hours a day, seven days a week. He didn't just make our bodies; His involvement continue moment after moment. As you read in an earlier chapter, every time we eat, He turns our food—dead stuff (fruit, meat, grains, leaves, *and* marshmallows) into fuel. When we inhale, He tells our bodies exactly what to do with the air we've just taken in. When our kids scrape their knees, His healing power goes into action and creates a scab so the wound has a protective covering. And when we fall into bed, completely depleted, we wake up the next morning feeling rested, because He restored us during the night. These actions are part of God's *ongoing* creative miracle in our bodies.

God is involved in the activities and events of our lives and in the world. He knows about everything. He grants His personal consent and orders its sequence. Sometimes His permission includes those things that look like all hell breaking loose for you and me. But as awful as the moment may seem to us, God is never surprised. Never. He knew this was coming. He has already been there.

He made us, and He's still involved.

God Is Merciful

Of all of God's attributes that we have described, it's His mercy that is the most comforting, especially when calamity knocks at our door. The fact that God is present provides solace and security. The fact that He is holy lifts our esteem for Him. The fact that He is the Creator expands our wonder. And the fact that He is sovereign assures us that life has order. It does not consist of a meaningless sequence of randomness.

It's God's mercy that fills our hearts with confidence.

But it's God's mercy that fills our hearts with confidence.

King David, who knew something about hell breaking loose, put this assurance into song:

> The LORD is merciful and gracious;
> > he is slow to get angry and full of unfailing love.
> He will not constantly accuse us,
> > nor remain angry forever.
> He has not punished us for all our sins,
> > nor does he deal with us as we deserve.
> For his unfailing love toward those who fear him
> > is as great as the height of the heavens above the earth.
> He has removed our rebellious acts
> > as far away from us as the east is from the west.
> The LORD is like a father to his children,
> > tender and compassionate to those who fear him.
> For he understands how weak we are;
> > he knows we are only dust.[10] *Psalm 103:8-14*

Although God has the right and the power to be merciless, especially when our disaster is of our own making, He is filled with love. He is sympathetic and patient with us.

The first thing to nail down is that God is God. This lays the foundation for being ready.

#2 The Bible Is God's Word

You'll remember that, with over 30 billion copies in print, the Bible is the best-selling book of all time. And best-selling books sell because of what? Buzz—people excitedly telling each other about them.

It was my privilege to grow up in a home where the Bible was valued, but the stories I read from *Foxe's Book of Martyrs* as a kid gave me a special reverence for God's Word. Real people—dads, moms, and kids—were burned at the stake because they refused to stop translating, printing, distributing, or reading the Bible. They would not deny its truth.

Persecution has not disappeared, even in a contemporary world. In 2006, only a few years after American and Coalition forces defeated the Taliban, giving Afghanistan freedom they had not known for generations, forty-one-year-old Abdul Rahman was arrested by Afghan authorities and sentenced to die. His crime? He owned a Bible. Most experts agreed that, without the outcry from the countries who had sacrificed to free Afghanistan, Rahman would have been beheaded. As it turned out, he was freed and immediately exiled to Italy on the grounds that he was mentally ill.

Nothing in Afghanistan was more dangerous than owning a copy of the Bible, including the possession of illegal drugs or explosives.

Why is this true? Because nothing is more dangerous than God's Word. It introduces people to the God who *is*. The Bible has the power to convict the guilty and to redeem the lost. It tells of fallen humanity bound for an eternity without hope, and a redeeming Savior. The Bible releases people from condemnation and provides a plan for escape from their captivity.

As critical as the directions shouted to people on the deck of a sinking ship, the Bible is God's indispensable instruction manual. It is His truth.

#3 Mankind Is Eternally Lost and in Need of a Savior

Stories about getting lost can be the stuff of great levity. But *being* lost is no laughing matter.

The message of mankind's universal lostness is a tough sell. We pack arenas to hear enthusiastic speakers tell us about our great untapped potential. Motivational materials are sold to aspiring businesspeople by the truckload.

Major corporations sponsor pep rallies to inspire their employees to productivity and increased sales.

Even clergymen are tempted to fill their churches by preaching a gospel of "you can do it" and "faith is fun and fulfilling and good for you." Lostness and sinfulness just don't market well.

But acknowledging our hunger brings you and me to the dinner table; confessing our sin lifts us to a Savior. This is an essential ingredient in our preparation for the inevitability of all hell breaking loose.

Ironically, the desperation and helplessness we might *feel*, especially in the middle of a crisis, is a *fact* all the time. Even when everything seems to be going along smoothly. Without a Savior, we're lost. Getting a promotion, buying a new car, celebrating a birthday with friends, winning the big game, becoming a parent for the first time—all these are wonderful experiences. But they can sometimes conceal our sense of lostness.

Cold weather is coming; pack your sweater. A hurricane is on its way; shutter your windows.

You and I are lost. We need a Savior.

#4 Jesus Christ Died to Redeem Mankind

Many years ago, some friends invited Bobbie and me to take their little boat, a Sunfish, and go sailing on Lake Michigan. If you have never seen one, a Sunfish is essentially a big surfboard with a large, triangular sail.

We were newlyweds, and I decided to go on this excursion without asking any questions. Basic questions like, "How does someone who has never sailed go about sailing?" I guess I didn't ask this because I was too eager to impress my bride. Not a good decision.

The day was clear, the breeze warm and just right for a small craft like ours. But the experience was a fiasco. I couldn't get the boat to do anything right. My frustration was eclipsed only by my embarrassment. Making some lame excuse for why the Sunfish refused to work properly, I put the boat back, and we went home.

The next day, the owner called to see how our adventure had gone. I admitted to "some frustration."

"Did you put down the centerboard?" the owner asked.

Not quick enough to mask my ineptness, I replied, "What centerboard?"

Jesus Christ is history's centerboard. Every time you and I write the date and year, we affirm this fact. Historical dates prior to His birth are recorded as "BC," or "before Christ." The years since His birth are referred to as "AD," or *anno Domini*—the year of our Lord. His coming to earth as a baby, split history.

> *Jesus' life, death, and resurrection provide us with eternal forgiveness for our sin— foundness for our lostness—and peace with a holy God.*

Today, Jesus provides stability and direction in the crosswinds and perils of life. He gives us steadiness, security, power, tranquility, and strength when all hell breaks loose.

Jesus' life, death, and resurrection provide us with eternal forgiveness for our sin—foundness for our lostness—and peace with a holy God. Life without Jesus is life without direction, without companionship . . . without a Savior.

Life without Jesus means facing tragedy without a centerboard.

#5 Grace and Faith Are Gifts

During the early days of my career, writing ad text and copy for the jackets and flaps of books was one of my assignments. The experience taught me to ask the question, "So what?"

If a customer or potential book buyer couldn't find the answer to the "So what?" question in the first sentence or two, it was back to the drawing board.

An honest, inquiring person could read that "God is God" and "the Bible is God's Word." He could be reminded that he is "lost and in need of a Savior" and that "Jesus Christ is God." Such a person could even agree that these things are true, and still he could ask, "So what?"

But receiving the gifts of faith and grace changes everything. With faith and grace, the information contained in the first four tenets becomes personal. The God of creation is my heavenly Father. God's Word tells me His story and uncovers the truth of my sin and salvation. My lostness drives me to Jesus Christ, who gave His life to be my Savior. I receive His grace. And like a place card on the table at a fancy dinner party, His grace has my name on it.

If this sounds self-centered, it's not. God's grace is meant to be poured into your heart first. Even the flight attendant tells you to put on your own oxygen mask before helping others with theirs.

But receiving this personalized gift of grace takes faith.

Jesus told the story of a woman—a widow—who had been wronged by an adversary. She went to a wicked judge and pleaded her own case. Day after day she ignored decorum, doing everything she could to gain the judge's attention. Try as he might, the petulant judge could not ignore her. The Bible actually says that the judge feared she would "wear him out" with her persistence.[11] So he relented and heard her case, granting her the equity she deserved.

Then Jesus said, "Learn a lesson from this evil judge. Even [though the judge was unjust,] he rendered a just decision in the end, so don't you think God will surely give justice to his chosen people who plead with him day and night? Will he keep putting them off? I tell you, he will grant justice to them quickly! But when I, the Son of Man, return, how many will I find who have faith?"[12] *Luke 18:6-8*

In telling the story, Jesus did not criticize the woman for pleading for herself and not for others. She laid claim to the judge's attention for her *own* case and believed that he would hear *her* petition. And Jesus called her persistence *faith*.

"I don't have that kind of faith," you might say. Of course, you don't. But God *will* give it to anyone who asks. Like grace, faith is a gift waiting to be received. And when we receive the gift of faith, truth becomes personal experience.

Here's how it happens. "For if you confess with your mouth that Jesus is Lord and believe in your heart that God raised him from the dead, you will be saved. For it is by believing in your heart that you are made right with God, and it is by confessing with your mouth that you are saved."[13] *Rom. 10:9-10*

#6 Belief and Works Are One

The argument has raged among biblical scholars throughout history. Is faith more important than good deeds, or are good deeds more important than faith?

The answer is yes.

What you and I believe cannot—and should not—be separated from how we act. What we claim as truth ought to have a visible impact on our behavior. Or as Don Quixote quipped, "The proof of the pudding is in the eating."[14]

"Show me your faith without your works," the apostle James said, echoing this idea, "and I will show you my faith *by* my works."[15]

As important as it is to believe in God and the Bible and Jesus, what is the value of these beliefs if our lives aren't in line, completely consistent? Our faith doesn't go dark when we're in a "heated discussion" with our spouse. This is where it should *show up*.

Our faith doesn't tiptoe away when we're out on the town with our friends. This is where it should *show up*.

We don't hit the delete key on our beliefs when we're sitting at our computer screen. This is where it should *show up*.

Our faith doesn't go dormant when all hell breaks loose. *This* is where it should show up.

"When the Holy Spirit controls our lives," Paul wrote, "*he* will produce this kind of fruit in us: love, joy, peace, patience, kindness, goodness, faithfulness, gentleness, and self-control."[16]

Living out this challenging list of characteristics doesn't make us believers. But if you and I *are* Christ-followers, our lives should be marked by this fully integrated, distinct behavior. And the work that's involved is not the gutting-it-out kind, like when we're jogging that last few hundred yards. The "work" is in turning over control to God's Holy Spirit—then He does the rest.

Like ingredients poured in a mixing bowl and "beaten to a thorough consistency," our beliefs and our works become indistinguishable from each other. What we believe takes over the way we think. And our thinking is transformed because we have received God's gift of faith. For example, the evidence that we have received this gift shows up in the way we speak and act to everyone, including our spouse and children.

No hidden camera would be able to contradict who we say we are. And even in the throes of the scenarios we talked about in the opening chapter, our behavior when all hell is breaking loose will be consistent with who you and I say we are—and how we act—in the ordinary.

This is really important. Before you give up and think, *I'm not really a Christian because I keep messing up*, listen to God's provision again. Because we have received God's gifts of grace and faith, we have the power to get back on track when we fail. We recognize God for who He is; we acknowledge that Jesus Christ's blood washes away our sin; we repent; we thankfully receive His grace and ask for His power to be and do what He wants.

#7 The Church Is God's Idea

So much of what we have discussed involves our individual beliefs and activities. But once the fundamentals are in place, the Christian life was never intended to be lived in isolation. Like a platoon attacking an enemy position in wartime, we have the muscle of joining fellow soldiers in our faith walk whether facing a crisis or celebrating together.

This is the church. Living in a special community of fellow revelers during the good times and surrounded by elite Special Forces when we're under fire is God's idea. "[As] iron sharpens iron, so one man sharpens another."[17]

Our local church is the place where we'll find this "iron."

James adds more of God's wisdom. "Confess your sins to each other," he writes, "and pray for each other so that you may be healed. The earnest prayer of a righteous person has great power and wonderful results."[18]

You and I will find "righteous" friends at church, people with whom we can band together, learn together, and grow together. These are the comrades who will pray for us, and for whom we will pray. The church is where we are taught truth and encouraged and strengthened and healed. Because of the church, you and I will never face tragedy without the comfort of people gathered around us to share in our pain.

In God's sovereign plan, Jesus Christ came to earth and gathered twelve men around Him to share in the experience of walking together. Jesus certainly was capable of accomplishing His task all by Himself. And no doubt there were times when the disciples got in the way. But Jesus set an example for how our journey with Him should be experienced, and it wasn't alone. It was in community.

In the same way that riding out a hurricane alone is a very bad idea, living out our lives in isolation will never work. The church is God's idea.

Always Be Ready

Many years ago, while preparing to teach the "seven things," I pretended that some neighbors had gotten a posse together. This group had come to our front door with a request.

"We know that you're a Christian," the spokesperson in the imagined scenario said when I answered the doorbell. "Most of us have dabbled in Christianity, but we would like to get serious and we'd like *you* to teach us about the basics of the Christian faith."

So the vision of this material was to make the core of Christian beliefs understandable and memorable and teachable.

The operating principle came from the apostle Peter's admonition in his first letter to the early church. "You must worship Christ as Lord of your life. And if you are asked about your Christian hope, always be ready to explain it."[19] Being able to respond to the imagined neighbors on our front porch motivated me to try to distill the basics into bite-size pieces. But helping others to be prepared to teach the same was even more exciting.

So let's say that the little troupe of neighbors is standing on *your* front porch. Their designated spokesperson is asking if *you* would be willing to tell them the basics of your Christian faith. Our discussion of the seven things has prepared you for this. You don't have to run for cover, desperately wishing someone else would answer the doorbell when your neighbors show up.

No, there's no need to run and hide. You're ready. Right now.

Another Kind of Ready

There's the sweater-in-your-suitcase ready, the storm-shutters ready, the building-on-rock ready. This is the kind of "ready" that the forecaster on the Weather Channel tells us to be when a storm is coming, the kind of "ready" that mounts a fire extinguisher in a very accessible place, the kind of "ready" that teaches our youngest child how to dial 911.

As wonderful as it will be when your neighbors do ring your doorbell and you're prepared to talk about your faith, there's another kind of "ready."

Ready is what you and I must be before all hell breaks loose. Ready with a well-equipped heart when crisis comes.

Of course, the great challenge is to syn-thetically put ourselves into the crisis mode before we're actually there. To *not* wait till it's too late to have these things nailed down, too late to launch our emergency plan, because we're in the middle of a disaster—and don't *have* a plan.

> Ready *is what you and I must be before all hell breaks loose.*

Following the attacks of September 11, 2001, U.S. senators and con-gressmen gathered on the Capitol steps. All hell had broken loose: two of the tallest buildings in the world lay in rubble, the Pentagon was smolder-ing, and a placid Pennsylvania field had become a heroes' graveyard.

The most powerful legislative body on the face of the earth would even-tually lay out a plan for a military response, but before that happened, they lifted their voices.

"God bless America," they sang, "land that I love. Stand beside her and guide her through the night with the light from above"[20]

Was this the pinnacle of collective naïveté, or was it the most important thing these powerful men and women could have done? Were these people capitulating to the enemy, or was asking God for help the most aggressive stand they could have taken—even more forthright than declaring war?

Being ready means that when crisis hits, we default not just to *something* that gets us through but to the *best thing* we could possibly think or do.

To the untrained eye, singing an old hymn about God's blessing on the Capitol steps in the wake of untold devastation may look like the tactic of a spineless nation. It's not.

Preparing ourselves for all hell breaking loose in our lives by nailing down a handful of ideas may look like an exercise in denial. It's not.

A New Kind of Dangerous

The most sobering and perilous dimensions of terrorist fear around the world are encapsulated in two words: *suicide bomber.*

Decades before we learned of this horrible wartime strategy, James A. Baldwin summarized the threat this way: "The most dangerous creation of any society is the man who has nothing to lose."[21]

In the Bible, Goliath the giant knew something about this sort of jeopardy. One morning in the Valley of Elah, this imposing warrior stood in shameless defiance to the army of the living God. Unfortunately for his army, Goliath had successfully defined the game. My might against your might. My armor versus yours.

Then along came a boy, armed with two weapons: a simple slingshot and nothing to lose.

"You come to me with a sword, a spear, and a javelin," David shouted to Goliath, "but I come to you in the name of the LORD of hosts, the God of the armies of Israel, whom you have taunted."[22]

David knew what you and I know.

Preparing ourselves for the hell that will come crashing down on us is only about one thing—holding on to what is true: what we know about God and His Word; what we believe about our lostness; our faith in the redemptive power of Jesus to save us; and the collective power of His people gathered together.

There is nothing else that we need. This is truth worth dying for.

In the face of the treachery that hunted him down, the apostle Paul announced his own coup de grace. His own defense against the peril that awaited him in prison or on the executioner's chopping block. "I myself no longer live," he said, "but Christ lives in me."[23] "Go ahead and *let* hell break loose," Paul defiantly declared. "You can't kill me. I'm already dead!"

When these truths are ours, you and I have everything to gain and nothing to lose, even during great crisis or unthinkable pressure.

As a boy, lying on my stomach behind the overstuffed chair and reading *Foxe's*, I was filled with admiration for the people who courageously faced their own deaths rather than succumb to the negotiations of their captors.

These martyrs joined many heroes who had gone before and became a cloud of witnesses to cheer me on.

> And what more shall I say? For the time would fail me to tell of Gideon and Barak and Samson and Jephthah, also of David and Samuel and the prophets: who through faith subdued kingdoms, worked righteousness, obtained promises, stopped the mouths of lions, quenched the violence of fire, escaped the edge of the sword, out of weakness were made strong, became valiant in battle, turned to flight the armies of the aliens.
>
> Others were tortured, not accepting deliverance, that they might obtain a better resurrection. Still others had trial of mockings and scourgings, yes, and of chains and imprisonment. They were stoned, they were sawn in two, were tempted, were slain with the sword. They wandered about in sheepskins and goatskins, being destitute, afflicted, tormented—of whom the world was not worthy.[24]

Fortified only with what they knew to be true and the faith to face hell itself, these people changed the course of history.

Now you and I will join them.

Acknowledgments

Until I entered the publishing business in 1976, I don't remember ever reading the acknowledgments in a book. As I recall, I quickly turned this page, along with the title page and the one with microscopic type including fascinating information like the Library of Congress Cataloging-in-Publication Data and ISBN number. This page turning gave me the sense of making early headway into the book.

But with over thirty years in the book business, I've read the acknowledgments page in nearly every book I've touched since.

In many ways, this page is a secret love letter to people whose names should probably appear on the cover, right along with the name of the author. So, with deepest gratitude, I want to thank . . .

My wife Bobbie. Please trust me, this is not the predictable thanks-to-my-wife nod. Bobbie is in every way my full writing companion. There isn't a single word or sentence in this book that she hasn't labored over with me. Where the book is clear and crisp and understandable, Bobbie gets the credit. If there are places where it's unclear, I won the argument and shouldn't have. Bobbie is a voracious student of the Bible and a trustworthy sounding board with every idea presented here. I'm so grateful to her.

My nephews, Andrew Wolgemuth and Erik Wolgemuth, to whom the book is dedicated. These men joined our firm several months before the writing began. And they covered early mornings for me for five months so I could keep my door shut and write. Thanks to Andrew and Erik and their wives, Chrissy and Kendal.

The Adventure Sunday school class in Nashville and the Upstream Sunday school class in Orlando who pulled this material out of their teacher. Classes filled with friends like Mark and Pam Oldham who experienced hell breaking loose in their own lives after having gone through this material. They lived to tell their story, which you'll find in the preface.

Friends whose names and stories you'll also read here, friends who have given me permission to tell you about their singular courage and faith. I'm deeply grateful for each one.

And other friends like Dr. Ken Boa and Ken Carpenter who read early drafts of the manuscript and lent their honest input.

Perhaps you've noticed that most publishing companies bear the name of people. There's a good reason since this is a partnership business. A lonely writer sits in front of his word processor (parchment, upright Royal typewriter, or legal pad), then hands the manuscript to his friend, the publisher. This person takes the draft manuscript, edits it, typesets it, packages it, catalogs it, manufactures it, and distributes it.

My friends at Thomas Nelson (see what I mean) were exactly that. Brian Hampton and Jonathan Merkh insisted that I write this book. Now I'm grateful. Bryan Norman, the managing editor—juggler—on the project, is sometimes like a man trying to manage the nursery at church. And on some days I'm the weeping and inconsolable two-year-old. Thank you, Bryan, for your tenderness, patience, and consummate professionalism. And to my friend, Tami Heim, who manages all the publishing divisions at Nelson. Thanks.

Belinda Bass for the great cover design (once again), Greg Stielstra who has forgotten more about book marketing than I'll ever know, Curt Harding, Brandi Lewis on the marketing team, and their boss, Jerry Park, whom I love like a brother.

The Nelson Sales team headed by Mark Schoenwald, the industry standard and dear friend. Gary Davidson, Scott Harvey, Rich Shear, and all the faithful men and women on the front lines. Thank you.

Mike Hyatt, Thomas Nelson's CEO, with whom I shared a brain—and a checkbook in our own business—for almost sixteen years. Mike is one of God's most precious gifts to me.

Finally, thanks to you (assuming you're still reading along). Of course, there's no way to know your situation or the reason why a book with this title has found its way into your hands. But it has. So my sincere prayer is that something you read here brings you helpful information, encouragement, and hope. Especially hope.

Thank you.

Notes

Introduction

1. John Rippon, "How Firm a Foundation," verse 4, *A Selection of Hymns from the Best Authors*, 1787.
2. In 1985, Julie went through major reconstructive surgery on her foot at Vanderbilt Children's Hospital.

Chapter 1

1. Google "Clutch Hitting" and you'll find page after page of entries that read more like NASA avionics than baseball. These folks are *serious* about clutch hitting.
2. 1 Kings 2:1–3
3. www.alienryderflex.dom/gyroscope/
4. John Foxe, *Foxe's Book of Martyrs* (1516–1587).
5. Hebrews 11:8–10
6. Hebrews 11:11–12
7. Hebrews 11:17–19
8. Hebrews 11:33
9. Hebrews 11:38
10. Acts 1:8
11. Acts 6:5
12. Ann Spangler and Robert Wolgemuth, *Men of the Bible: A One-Year Devotional Study of Men in Scripture* (Grand Rapids: Zondervan, 2003), 427.
13. Ibid.
14. John Rippon, "How Firm a Foundation," verse 3, *A Selection of Hymns from the Best Authors*, 1787.

Chapter 2

1. Exodus 3:6
2. Exodus 3:14. In most translations these words are capitalized, as seen here. Most scholars agree that this was because God did not lower His voice when He said these words. No further explanation should be necessary.
3. 2 Chronicles 16:9 NLT
4. Genesis 1:1 KJV
5. Ephesians 1:4
6. Psalm 19:1 NIV
7. Quentin Smith, "Big Bang Cosmology and Atheism: Why the Big Bang Is No Help to Theists," *Free Inquiry* magazine 18, no. 2, available at www.secularhumanism.org/index.php?section=library&page=smith_18_2.
8. Derek Parfit, "Why Anything? Why This?" *London Review of Books*, January 22, 1998, 24.
9. James MacDonald, *Downpour: He Will Come to Us Like the Rain* (Nashville: Broadman & Holman Publishers, 2006), 50.

10. 1 Timothy 6:15–16

11. Isaiah 6:4–5

12. Mark 4:39

13. Mark 4:35–40

14. 1 Kings 19:11–12 (emphasis added)

15. Stuart Hamblen, "How Big Is God?" from the album, *Of God I Sing* (Canyon Country, California, 1962).

16. Although the next chapter addresses people who see the world this way, let me at least say here that I do not believe these scholars are unintelligent. I'm often stunned by their brilliance when I read their writings. I do, however, believe that they are wrong, because I believe that, without faith, they are lost.

17. Ephesians 2:8–9

18. Job 42:2, 5

19. Psalm 103:13–14 NIV

20. 2 Chronicles 7:3

21. Jonah 4:2

22. Ephesians 2:4–5

23. 2 Corinthians 5:14 (emphasis added)

Chapter 3

1. Russell Ash, *The Top Ten of Everything 2002* (New York: Penguin Books Ltd. 2001).

2. My other writings include: the notes to *The Devotional Bible for Dads* (Grand Rapids: Zondervan, 1998); *What's in the Bible* with Dr. R. C. Sproul (Nashville: W Publishing Group, 2000); *Men of the Bible*, with Ann Spangler (Grand Rapids: Zondervan, 2003); and *Fathers of the Bible* (Grand Rapids: Zondervan, 2006).

3. Foxe, *Foxe's Book of Martyrs*, chap. 12.

4. Ibid.

5. Some contemporary Roman Catholic scholars believe that the clergy of Tyndale's day were also concerned about what they perceived as inaccuracies in Tyndale's translation. But they don't argue that their sixteenth-century colleagues could have been a bit more diplomatic with him.

6. Foxe, *Foxe's Book of Martyrs*, chap. 15.

7. Marvin J. Rosenthal, *Zion's Fire* magazine, March/April 2006, 5.

8. This is why many evangelical scholars and teachers lay claim to the absolute accuracy of the Bible, "in its original manuscripts." Apparently, the authors of the Bible books were divinely inspired by the Holy Spirit. The scribes were ordinary folks, doing their best.

9. F. F. Bruce, *The New Testament Documents* (Grand Rapids: Wm. B. Eerdmans Publishing Company, 2003), 11.

10. James MacDonald, *God Wrote a Book* (Wheaton, IL: Crossway Books, 2002), 20.

11. Norman Geisler and William Nix's, *A General Introduction to the Bible: Revised and Expanded Edition* (Chicago: Moody Press, 1986), 408.

12. You will find Norman Geisler and William Nix's *A General Introduction to the Bible* (Chicago: Moody Press, 1968) helpful in giving specific detail on how these disparate manuscripts came together as the Bible we now read.

13. Psalm 72:9

14. Psalm 72:10, 15

15. Isaiah 9:6

16. Isaiah 7:14

17. Micah 5:2

18. Genesis 2:24–25

19. Ephesians 5:21–22, 25; 6:1–2, 4 NIV

20. Colossians 3:22–23; 4:1

21. James 2:8–9

22. Matthew 25:37–40

23. Philippians 4:12 NIV

24. Luke 16:10–13 NIV

25. 1 Timothy 6:10 NIV

26. P. T. Barnum, *The Art of Money Getting* (Whitefish, MT: Kessinger Publishing Company, 2004), 12.

27. Benjamin Rush, *Essays: Literary, Moral and Philosophical*, "A Defence of the Use of the Bible as a School Book" (1798), 94, available at http://deila.dickinson.edu/cgi–bin/docviewer.exe?CISOROOT=/ownwords&CISOPTR=19843.

28. Look at the University crests of Harvard, Yale, and Princeton.

29. Joshua 1:8–9

30. 2 Timothy 3:16–17

31. John 8:31–32

32. C. S. Lewis, *The Problem of Pain* (1940; repr., New York: HarperCollins, 2001), 91.

33. Psalm 34:18 NASB (emphasis added)

34. Job 5:17–18

35. Psalm 143:8

36. Psalm 32:8

37. SKG: Steven Spielberg, Jeffrey Katzenberg, David Geffen.

Chapter 4

1. Psalm 51:5 NASB

2. Actually, long before country music co-opted the place, the Ryman was first the home of the Union Gospel Tabernacle—thus the country music connection to a church.

3. John Kramp *Out of Their Faces and into Their Shoes* (Nashville: Broadman & Holman, 1995).

4. John MacArthur, *The MacArthur Bible Commentary* (Nashville: Thomas Nelson Publishers, 2005), 844.

5. Jeremiah 17:5 NIV

6. Jeremiah 17:9

7. Robert Robinson, "Come Thou Fount," *A Collection of Hymns Used by the Church of Christ in Angel Alley, Bishopgate*, 1759.

8. James MacDonald, *Downpour: He Will Come to Us Like the Rain* (Nashville: Broadman & Holman Publishers, 2006), 26.

9. Romans 3:10–11 NIV

10. The NFL rules have changed since Jack Tatum tackled Darryl Stingley. Using the top of the helmet as the first point of contact—spearing—carries with it a 15-yard penalty—even immediate ejection if the referee interprets the hit as flagrant.

11. Mark 10:22 KJV

12. Mark 10:17 NIV

13. "You're So Vain," words and music by Carly Simon, Copyright 1972, Quackenbush Music, Ltd., All rights reserved. By the way, Carly never disclosed who she had in mind when she recorded it. Rumors say she was poking fun at Mick Jagger, Kris Kristofferson, Cat Stevens, or Warren Beatty, who reputedly called to personally thank her for the song.

14. Proverbs 16:18 NIV

15. Luke 18:9 NIV

16. See Luke 18:11–13

17. John 5:6

18. John 5:7

Chapter 5

1. Herod returned the favor by constructing a temple to the god Pan, in Caesar's honor—a massive construction project with ornate niches cut into the sheer limestone cliff walls surrounding the region. These were used as altars to Pan, his father Hermes, and other gods of the day.

2. Matthew 16:13–17

3. Matthew 16:20

4. Mark 1:44

5. Mark 1:45 NCV

6. John 10:23–24

7. John 10:30

8. John 14:6

9. Mark 10:18

10. In French medieval times, a man would remove a glove—a gauntlet—and throw it on the ground in front of an opponent as a symbol that a challenge was being offered.

11. C. S. Lewis, *Mere Christianity* (1952; repr., New York: HarperCollins, 2001), 52.

12. Ibid., 197.

13. In Athens they even erected an altar with the inscription "To the Unknown God." Already worshiping a plethora of deities, they built this altar just in case they had missed one.

14. Hebrews 1:1–4

15. Matthew 3:7–9 NLT

16. Joel 2:13 NLT

17. Matthew 3:11–12 NLT

18. John 10:30

19. Colossians 1:19

20. John 1:3

21. Colossians 1:15–16

22. Exodus 20:4–5

23. Exodus 33:18–22

24. Exodus 34:30

25. Leon Wieseltier, "Mel Gibson's Lethal Weapon. The Worship of Blood," *The New Republic Online*, February 26, 2004, https://ssl.tnr.com/p/docsub.mhtml?i=20040308&s=wieseltier030804.

26. Andy Rooney, *60 Minutes*, CBS, February 22, 2004.

27. Isaiah 53:3

28. 1 Corinthians 4:9–10 NIV

29. Hebrew 1:3 (emphasis added)

30. Matthew 11:28 NIV

Chapter 6

1. 2 Corinthians 9:15

2. Titus 3:4–5 NIV

3. Ephesians 2:8–9 NIV (emphasis added)

4. Hebrews 11:6 NIV

5. Matthew 28:10 NIV

6. Luke 24:16 NASB (emphasis added)

7. Luke 24:31 (emphasis added)

8. Mark 9:22–24

9. Luke 15:17–20 NIV

10. Luke 15:17 NCV

11. Psalm 51:3–4 NASB

12. Rev. Colin Smith is the senior pastor of the Arlington Heights (Illinois) Evangelical Free Church and the author of several books including the four-book series, *Unlocking the Bible* (Chicago: Moody Publishers, 2002).

13. James 3:3–5 NASB

14. Romans 10:9–10 (emphasis added)

15. Ravi Zacharias, *Walking from East to West* (Grand Rapids: Zondervan, 2006).
16. Ibid.
17. Luke 15:20 NASB
18. Luke 15:22–24 (author's translation)
19. Luke 8:22 NIV
20. Luke 8:25 NIV
21. Matthew 11:28 NASB
22. Matthew 16:17 NCV
23. Luke 11:9–10

Chapter 7

1. James 2:14–17, 26 NIV
2. 1 Corinthians 10:31
3. Matthew 5–7
4. Romans 12:9–16 NLT
5. Titus 3:4–5 NIV
6. Titus 2:11–12 NIV
7. These groups were called *Anabaptists* (which means "baptizing again") because of their reaction to Martin Luther's belief in baptizing babies. The Anabaptists did not consider a person technically baptized until, as adult believers, they were immersed in water.
8. 2 Corinthians 6:17 KJV
9. To ensure uniformity to the code, some Mennonites spray painted the chrome—grilles, hubcaps, and bumpers—on their cars . . . Black Bumper Mennonites.
10. Luke 10:25–36 NLT
11. 1 Peter 2:9–12 NIV
12. Matthew 7:1–5
13. Romans 8:38–39
14. 2 Corinthians 5:17 NLT
15. George Washington, first inaugural address, Thursday, April 30, 1798.
16. 1 Corinthians 10:31

Chapter 8

1. More than once during construction, I was charged with the job of pick-axing through the reluctant stuff in order to pour footings for the foundations.
2. Matthew 16:18
3. Many historians believe that the apostle Thomas traveled east to India as a missionary.
4. R. C. Sproul and Robert Wolgemuth, *What's in the Bible* (Nashville: W Publishing Group, 2000).
5. Hebrews 9:11
6. Genesis 12:1–3
7. Jacob's name was changed to Israel after an all-night wrestling match with an angel.
8. Before Isaac's birth, God changed Abram's name to Abraham, and Sarai's name to Sarah.
9. Exodus 25:8–9
10. Hebrews 10:25 NLT
11. 1 Corinthians 12:12–14, 20, 26–27
12. 1 John 1:3
13. Unlike any pregame performance of "The Star–Spangled Banner," Whitney Houston's presentation was released as a single and raced to Billboard's charts.
14. Composed by C. Herbert Woolston (1856–1927).

15. 1 Corinthians 5:1–2, 6, 12–13 NLT. Other examples of church discipline are described in Titus 3:10, 2 Thessalonians 3:6, Romans 16:17, and Matthew 18.

16. Michael Kunzelman, Associated Press, February 16, 2006.

17. Ibid.

18. Ephesians 6:12 NLT

19. Vernon J. Charlesworth, "A Shelter in the Time of Storm," 1880.

Chapter 9

1. Matthew 7:24–27 NCV

2. The words to the hymn "The Solid Rock" were written in 1834 by Edward Mote, a Baptist pastor who served for twenty-six years in Sussex, England.

3. Luke 15:8–11

4. Philippians 3:13–14

5. Philippians 3:13 NASB

6. Lewis, *Mere Christianity*, 192.

7. The south tower was struck by United Airlines Flight 175 at 9:02 and collapsed at 9:59. The Pentagon was hit by American Airlines Flight 77 at 9:37, and United Airlines Flight 93 crashed into a Pennsylvania field at 10:03. The carnage at the north tower book-ended the one and three-quarter hours that morning that will never be forgotten. The timeline for these horrific events can be seen at www.webenglish.com.tw/ encyclopedia/en/wikipedia/s/se/september_11__2001_attacks_timeline_for_the_day_of_the_a.html.

8. Psalm 46:1–2 NLT

9. Ephesians 2:10

10. Psalm103:8–14 NLT

11. Luke 18:5 NASB

12. Luke 18:6–8 NLT

13. Romans 10:9–10 NLT

14. Miguel de Cervantes Saavedra, *Don Quixote de la Mancha*, 1605.

15. James 2:18 (emphasis added)

16. Galatians 5:22–23 NLT (emphasis added)

17. Proverbs 27:17 NASB

18. James 5:16 NLT

19. 1 Peter 3:15 NLT

20. Irving Berlin, "God Bless America."

21. James A. Baldwin, *Collected Essays* (New York: Library of America, 1998), 330.

22. 1 Samuel 17:45 NASB

23. Galatians 2:20 NLT

24. Hebrews11:32–38